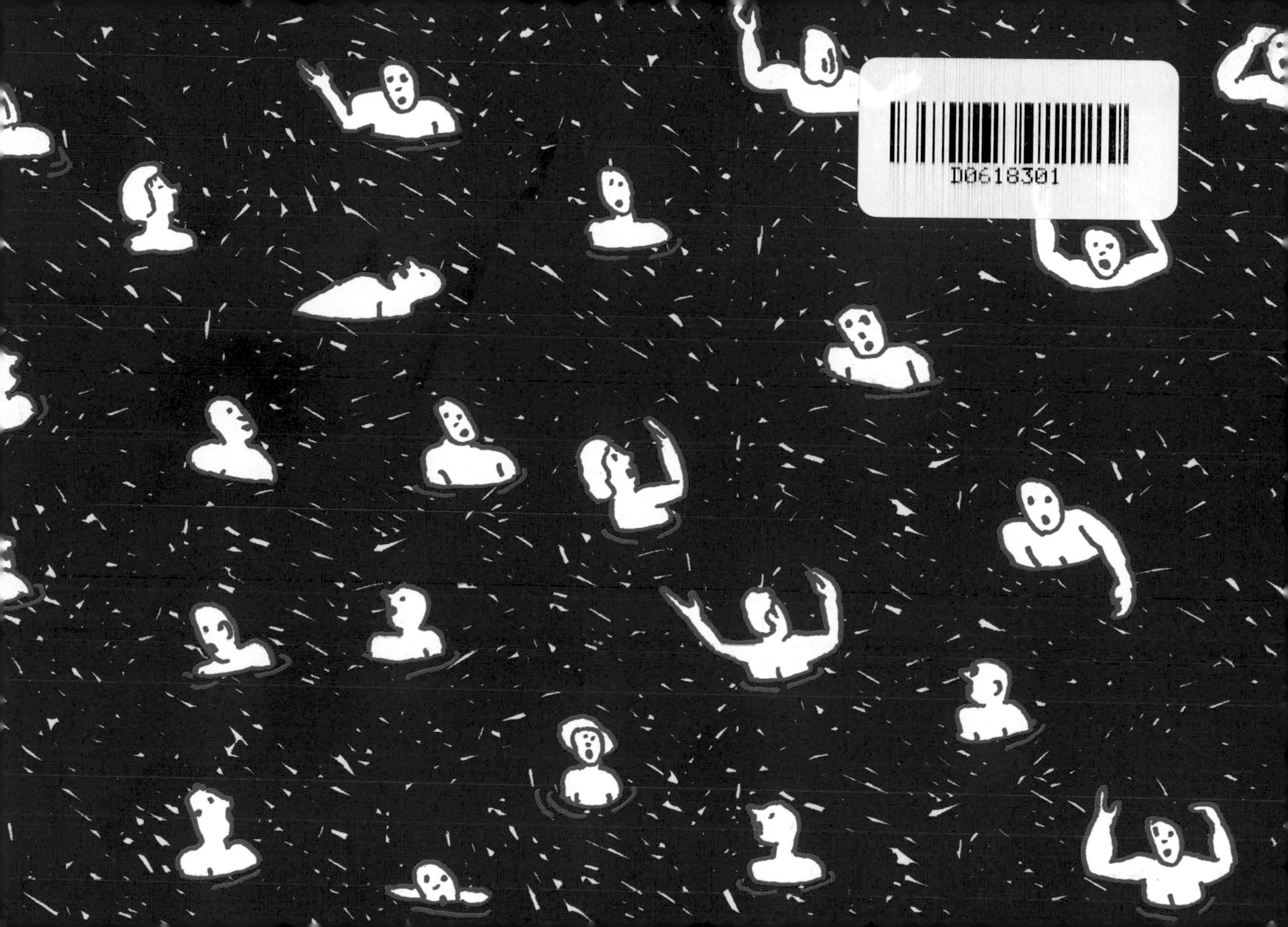

HELL

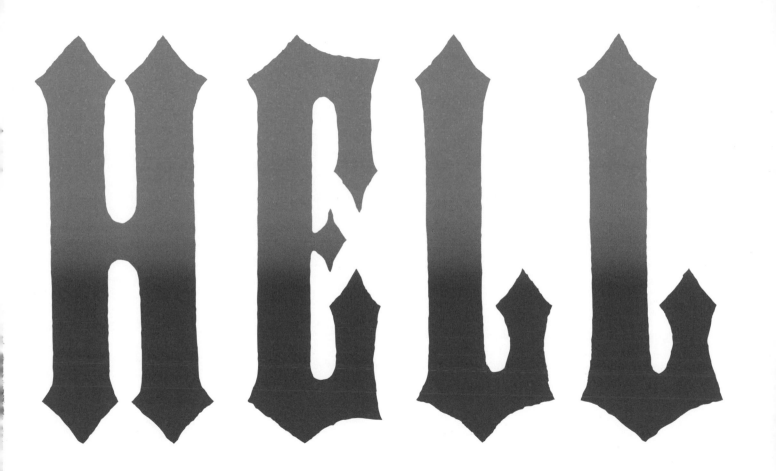

HELL

THE PEOPLE AND PLACES

SEYMOUR CHWAST STEVEN HELLER

PA PRESS   PRINCETON ARCHITECTURAL PRESS · NEW YORK

FIRE, BRIMSTONE AND OTHER UNPLEASANTRIES

Doomed to eternal damnation are those who accede to an irrepressible calling to comprehend the incomprehensible thus defying the dictum that cautions one to allow the sleeping dogs of hell to sleep undisturbed.

Like Virgil did so well, we too guide you through the realms of hell and purgatory; We rashly yet willingly decided to take the perilous journey through a portal most dangerous, through the gates of hell. Inspired by Dante's *Divine Comedy: The Inferno* and dozens of other guides and manuals, secular and religious, cult and occult into the darkness. We seek to find, if possible, how many of these damnable hot spots exist or have existed in the extra-dimensional and intra-spiritual worlds that hold sway over body and mind. We have accepted this mission with full acknowledgment of the possible consequences—of becoming forever enslaved by Garm and Lucifer (or whatever one chooses to call the guardians of these underworlds).

Like the universe, hell is infinite. Like a planet, hell nonetheless has shape and form. Hell is both beyond comprehension and unequivocally real in the humanoid mind.

CONTENTS

INTRODUCTION

WARNING: This book is not affiliated with any specific religion, sect or cult and neither supports nor rejects the concept of hell as the roasting pan of human existence.

The word "hell" comes from Old English *hel* or *helle,* referring to the under- or netherworld of the dead where hoary souls reside. If you are, however, interested in knowing more about the etymology, you do not need this book for that—just google it on your own. Yet once you have entered the bowels of internet data, a linked-in conflagration of information designed to stir your conscious and tempt your unconscious (or the other way around), you could easily fall into a bottomless abyss for which there is no escape button. Many would say that seeking out certain knowledge is a kind of hell; a place—real or imagined—where every click of a button, swipe of a screen or activation of a voice will trap you like so many endless corridors in the everlasting labyrinth from which there is no return. Your punishment, so to speak, for wanting to know the meaning, let alone the experience, of hell is to become its shrouded prisoner—a slave to the delights of torment.

There are so many hells, each torturous in its own particular manner, yet they have one thing in common: all are eternal penalties overseen by one or more craggy spirits. The contexts they may derive from are mystical, mythological and occult and never scientific. Hell has no tangible reality; it comes up from the darkest region of the subconscious and inhabits realities as they are accepted at any given time. There is no universal hell; not all hells fit all people. They come in different sizes and with unique rituals. Not every sentient being (or thing?) perceives the exact same grand plan for an afterlife, although there are plenty of similarities between them all. Not all hells are hidden from view, covered in smoke and flame. Some are in full view and admission is free.

Without hell there would be no heaven. Without heaven there would be no hell. This, however, is not a shared truth. But it is not necessary to discuss the concept of heaven—a concept that also comes in different sizes—to address hell or its over- and underlords. Hell lives on guilt. Hell feeds on superstition. Hell is nourished by weakness.

If your hand causes you to sin, cut it off. It is better for you to enter life maimed than with two hands to go into hell, where the fire never goes out.

—Mark 9:43

7

Hell is not solely supernatural—it is as natural as the concepts of good and bad. Hell is preordained, imposed and circumstantial.

A personal hell: Growing up with Heller as my name allowed childhood friends and enemies the opportunity to practice a little wordplay at my expense. There was not much talk of hell in my secular household. If I misbehaved, my Orthodox Jewish grandmother (and even my Reformed Jewish mother) might utter, "God will punish you for that," resulting in the inevitable or conveniently coincidental stubbing of my toe or the like, proving their point. But never did I ever hear any family say, "You will go to hell for that," or speaking of a particularly unpleasant person, "I hope he [or she] burns in hell."

Hell was not the curse of choice in my life but it is certainly the ultimate in damnation for many peoples, religions, nations and believers of all types. While hell for me was a joke—someone, a demon of sorts, joking, for example, that I "should go to Heller" (take a guess how many times have I heard that devilishly funny quip)—for those who righteously live life on earth only so they can earn entry into the hereafter, whatever and wherever that may be, hell is hell! It is the ultimate punishment for the worst of crimes at the time of death. By that I mean, crimes of one era are not always crimes of another and sins from then are not always sins from now. Not everyone, even those who believe in the same deity or dogma, will accept the same transgressions. Every era, epoch, generation, situation, etc., has its own guidelines—what's more certain of them have indulgences available (like Get Out of Hell Free cards) that will alter the ruling.

Whereas the statutes governing differing concepts of heaven are fairly similar, for hell the edicts that enable admission are likely to shift as do the sands of time. Still, the general idea of hell is that it constitutes a very bad place for very bad people from which there is usually no hope of redemption. Yet redemption is built into many religions. Some religions allow believers to buy their way out of hell, while others are willing to give a free pass to the truly repentant.

Whatever is said about the accommodations, hell does not exclude or redline. Everyone is welcome. There is enough room for all who have earned their rightful place. Hell is an autocracy, but everyone is treated equally; given the state of the earthly life, there is something to be said in its favor.

Steven Heller

here hell began is hard to say, or where it ends, or whether it exists at all. Hell is a human construct, an idea or superstition, conceived millennia ago by man. There are enough underworld deities to fill hell and beyond. The following is a guide to the top satanic — the hottest (and in some cases, coldest) — demimondes to be found at the core of human imagination.

HEBREW GEHENNA

"There is no concrete Jewish vision of the afterlife," stated Rabbi Shalom Carmy, Yeshiva University professor of Jewish studies and philosophy and author of *Jewish Perspectives on the Experience of Suffering*. But if there were an afterlife, one of its more concrete locales would be found in Jerusalem, below the Old City walls, where a ravine that begins as a gentle, grassy separation between hills descends south into the rocky earth. Eventually the ravine becomes a steep, craggy depth, scarred on its far side by shallow caves and pits pocked by hollowed-out chambers and narrow crypts. Gehenna is a gruesome place where people burn their garbage and where cadavers are burned as well. Early Christians claimed it was here that the sinful were choked and incinerated. The smell of burning offal was intense.

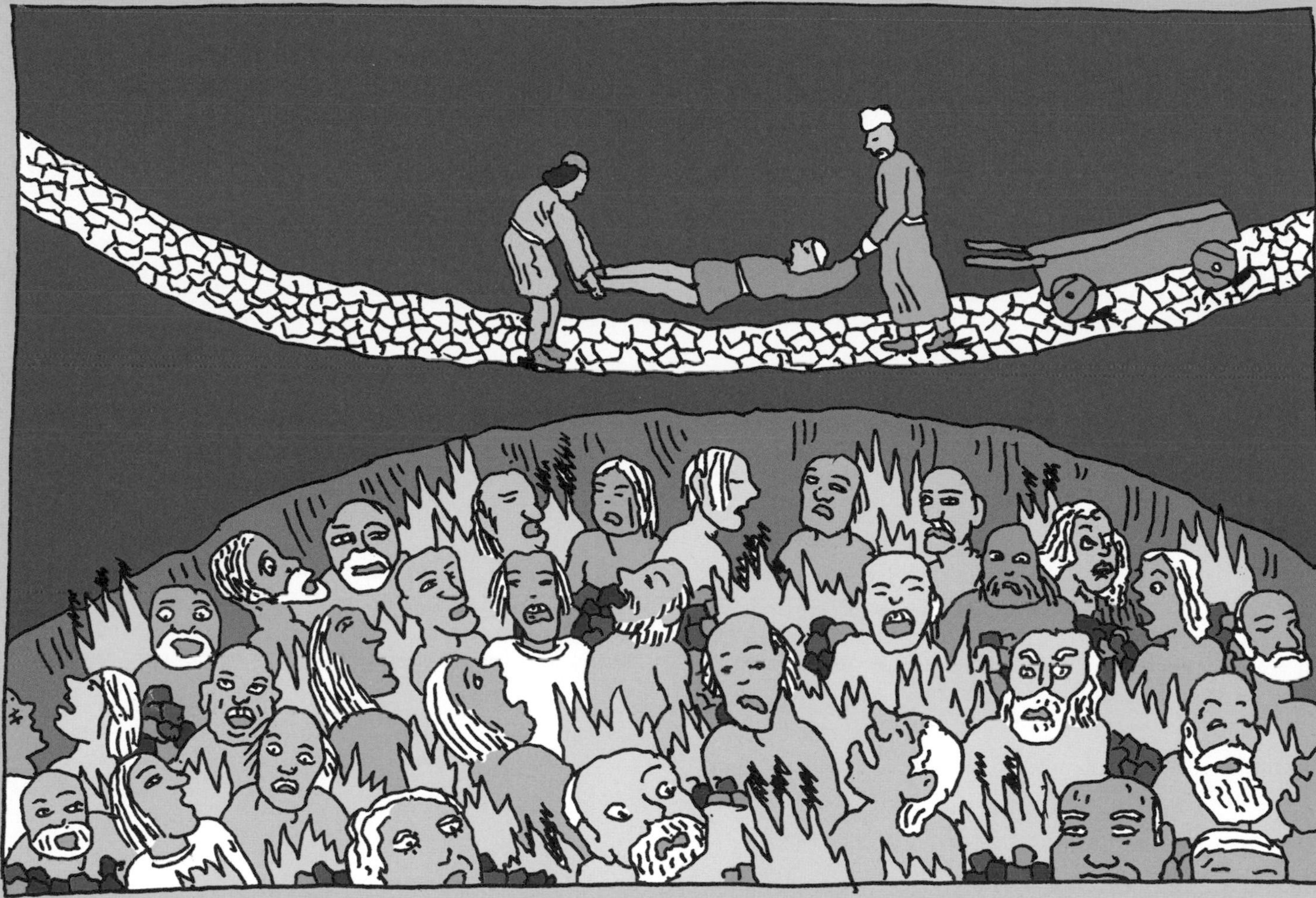

Islam Underworld

Jahannam is the Islamic hell. According to teachings, the fate of a soul is the result of its own actions. Those who have defied the will of Allah "can blame only themselves." Hell is located under al-Ṣirāṭ, the name of the right way, the straight path of success in the hereafter, and only Allah can allow passage to paradise. Come Judgment Day, souls must hastily cross over a narrow bridge to the next world. While many among the sinners are destined to fall into the flaming pit below, spending all eternity consumed in fire, many others make it across unharmed, or with barely a burn or threat of eternal discomfort.

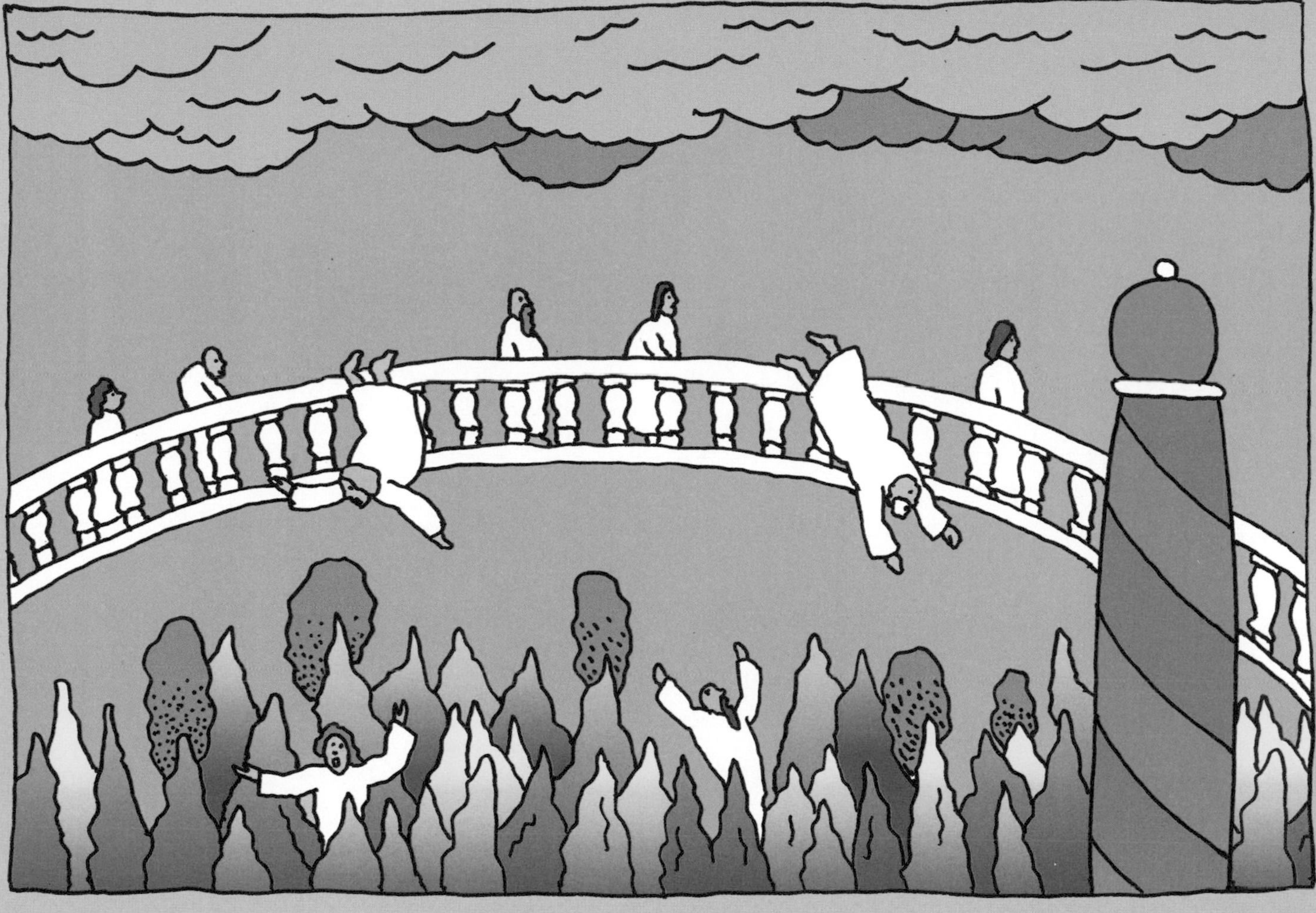

Jahannam in Sunni Islam

In Jahannam, the skin of sinners is burned yet regenerated so they will continue to suffer for eternity. In this horrific realm of retribution, anguish is the norm and punishment depends on seven different degrees of evil:

- Fire for Muslim sinners.
- Inferno interim for Christian sinners.
- (Provisional) purgatory for Jewish sinners.
- Burning fire for renegades.
- Imprisonment for witches and fortune tellers.
- Furnace for disbelievers.
- Bottomless pit for hypocrites.

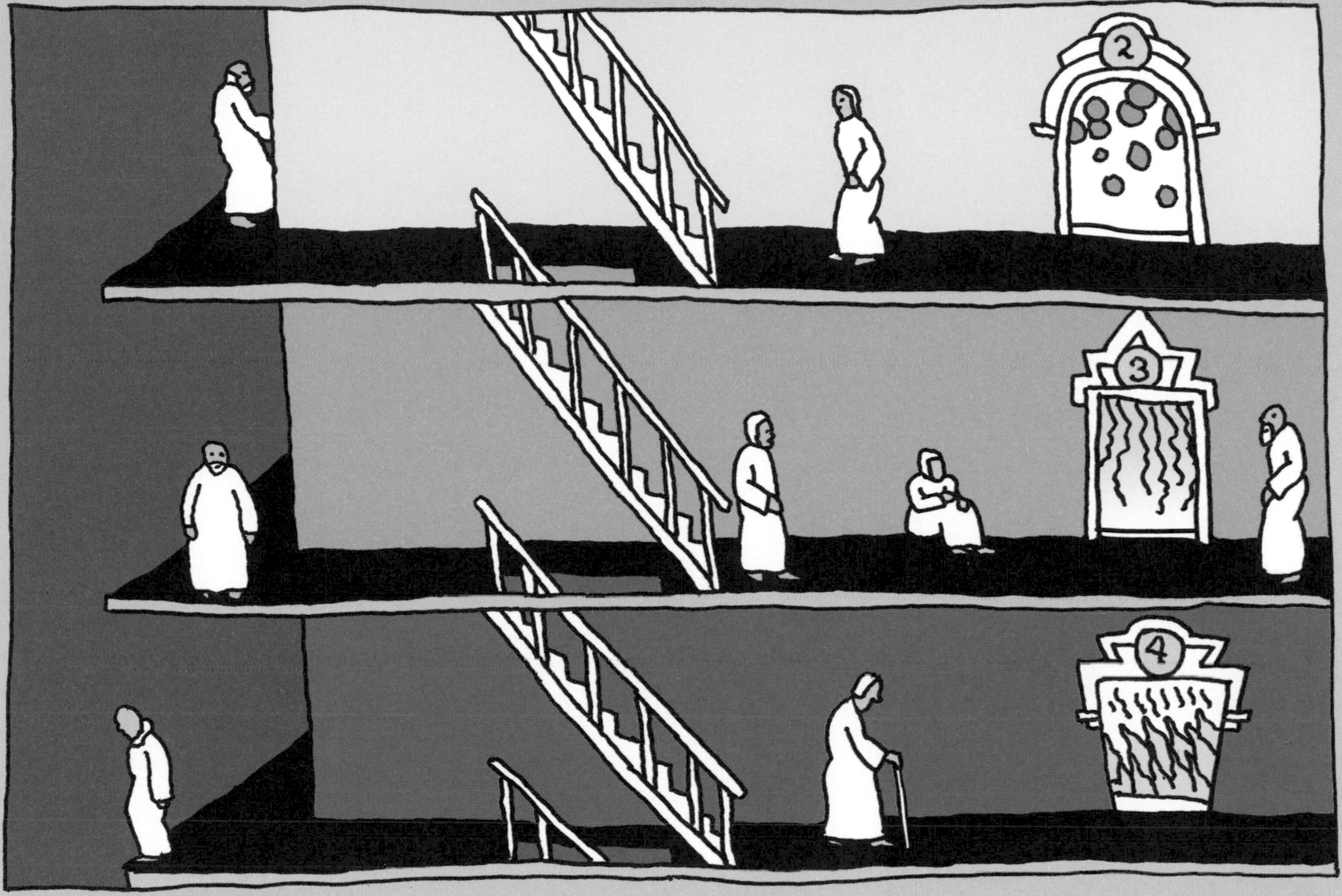
2
3
4

Sheol

Sheol, a place of death, is referred to in the Hebrew Bible as a place of darkness to which the dead go and souls are cut off from God. It is divided into two parts: one for the wicked who have sinned against God, the other for those who lived exemplary lives. During the time of the Second Temple (500 BC–70 AD), Sheol was the home of the wicked while paradise was the home of the righteous dead until the Last Judgment. It is equated with Gehenna in the *Talmud*.

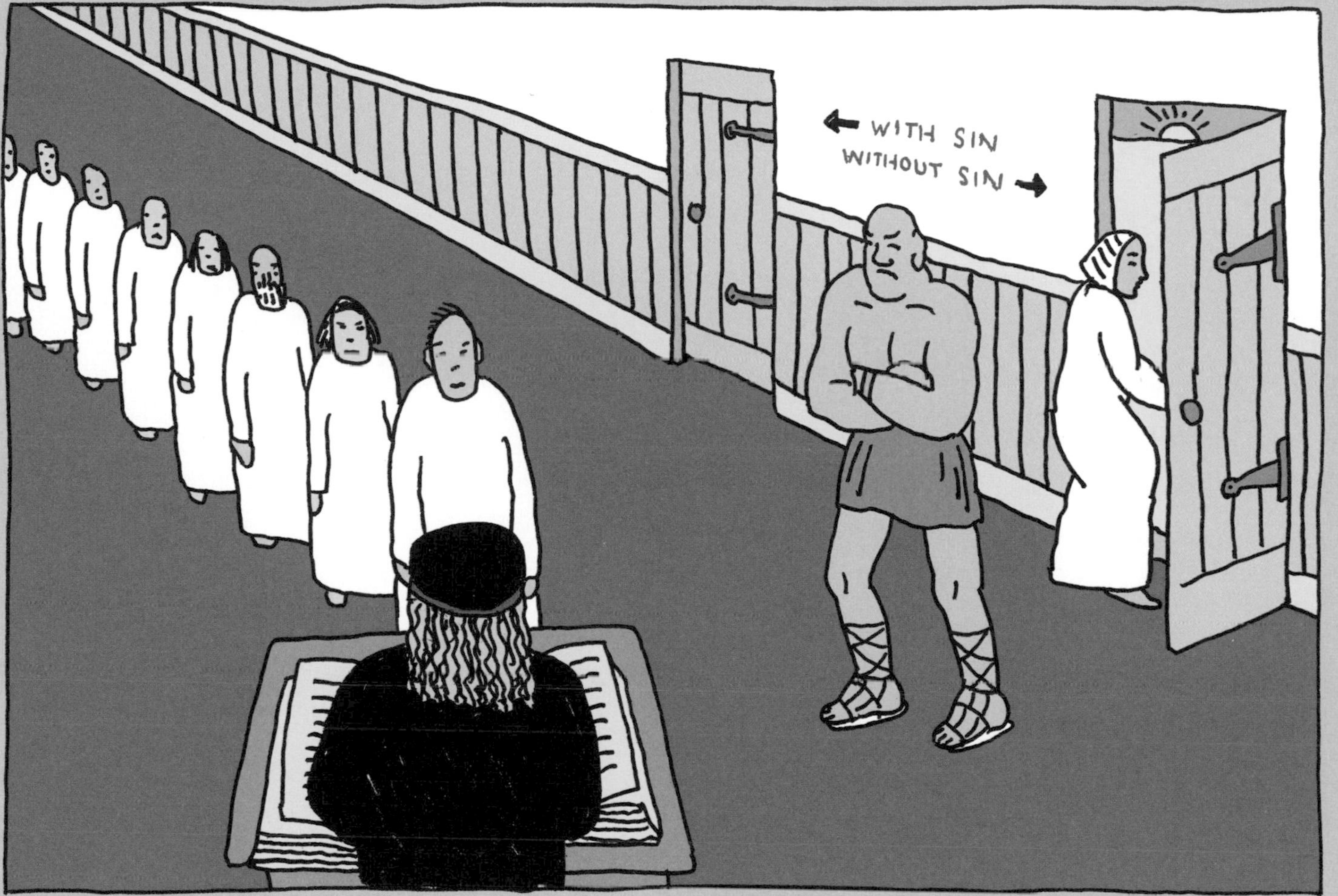

WITH SIN
WITHOUT SIN

THE KORAN

The Koran tells of the travels of Muhammad, Islam's prophet, in heaven and hell and of what awaits nonbelievers. Souls have a choice of observing the truth or following Iblīs (Satan). The Last Judgment will occur when souls will be presented to Allah, who hopes for salvation for all. Infidels, however, must suffer Islamic hell. Those in the hottest part of hell are steeped in fire and boiling water. They are bound in liquid pitch to enhance the burning. Those that drink the boiling water suffer greatly as lungs, stomach and intestines are torn apart. Those who try to escape are beaten with maces of iron.

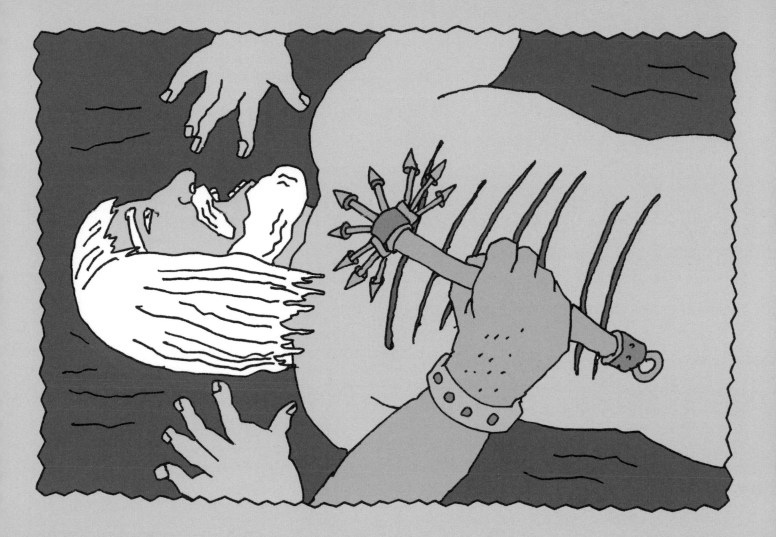

Gnosticism

Gnostics (the word *gnosis* means "secret knowledge") were groups of early Christian cult followers and were heretics who believed that hell was present in the materialism of daily life on earth. Their Gnostic gospels argue that an alien, unknowable god created a clear light, or "upper heaven," but mistakenly allowed for the Demiurge, or "lower god," to be creator of the world, matter and human beings. Heaven was unassailable while the world, comprising humans, was inherently evil and gross. Some Gnostics thought Jesus was a human. Christians believed he was divine. A third-century myth quotes Jesus telling Mary Magdalene the underworld is a huge dragon that completely surrounds the world. Inside the dragon are twelve dungeons where torture is performed with demons that terrorize the dead. Christ's second coming ensures that the human race is doomed. Christ is said to have said that "Death is coming. Life is foreplay."

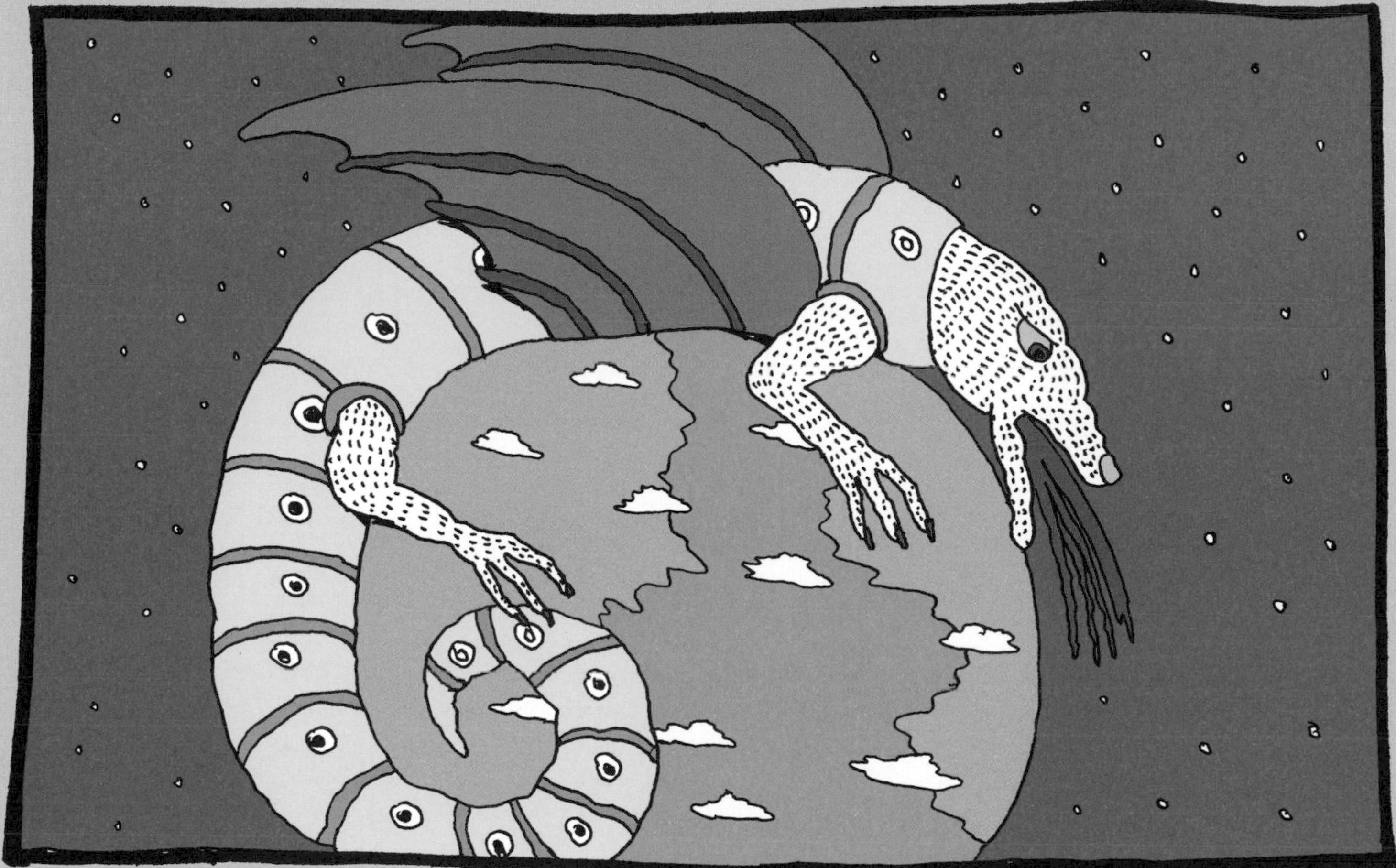

THE TEACHING OF MANICHAEISM

MIDDLE EAST

Manichaeism combines Christian, Gnostic and pagan elements with the idea that there are two gods. The prophet Mani, a third-century Persian from Assyria, was the founder of Manichaeism and preached the dualistic religion with two gods: the god of light associated with the kingdom of heaven, angels and the beauties of nature; the god of darkness who identified with demons, the materialistic world, fire, smoke, bad weather and women.

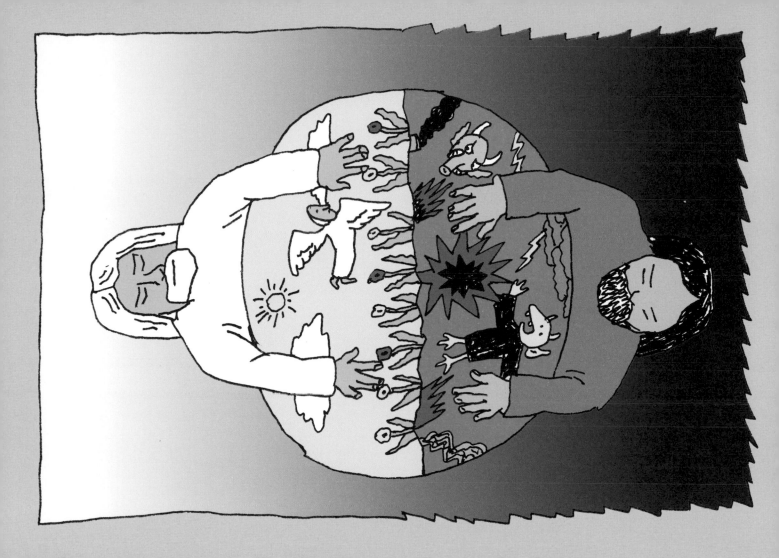

ZOROASTRIAN SCRIPTURES

Zoroastrianism is a faith established by the Persian prophet Zoroaster, or Zarathustra, somewhere between 1500 and the sixth century BC. The teachings in the sacred scriptures state that two twin deities representing good and evil battle for world control. *The Book of Ardā Wīrāz*, a fundamental Zoroastrian text, tells the story of a journey into the next world and includes descriptions of hell, called the "House of Lies," as a place of evil thoughts, evil deeds and darkness. The book describes 85 punishments for those who spoke falsehoods, lies and profanity. The Crossing of the Chinvat Bridge is when all dead souls must face a reckoning for the actions committed during their lifetime. If evil deeds dominate, the spirit is condemned to a deep abyss, seized by the demon Vizarsh and then tortured until the apocalypse. But there is redemption: the wicked, once destroyed by molten metal to purify their souls, are in turn allowed to enter heaven.

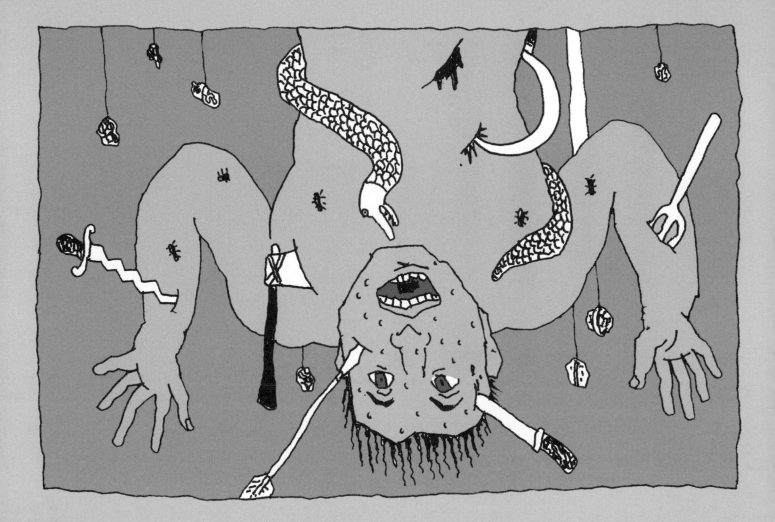

ERESHKIGAL

Ereshkigal, the Sumerian mistress of the dead and ruler of Aralu, the "Land of No Return," has received the underworld as her share of creation, while her sister Inanna is the goddess of beauty and fertility and the queen of heaven. Aralu is a dimension of eternal darkness, a communal burying ground where spirits eat only dust and suffer, a dry barren place below the "sweet waters of the underground." The dead are not punished nor rewarded by their deeds in life; all souls go to the same afterlife and their condition is determined by the lavishness of their burial and the devotion of their descendants. Hell is called the "Great Palace"; Nergal is a minor god, who has rendezvous with the dead Ereshkigal and later marries her. He reigns in her palace, on the watch for lawbreakers, and guards over the fount of life lest any of her subjects take of it and so escape her rule. Ereshkigal's offspring and servant is Namtar, the evil demon, a.k.a. Death.

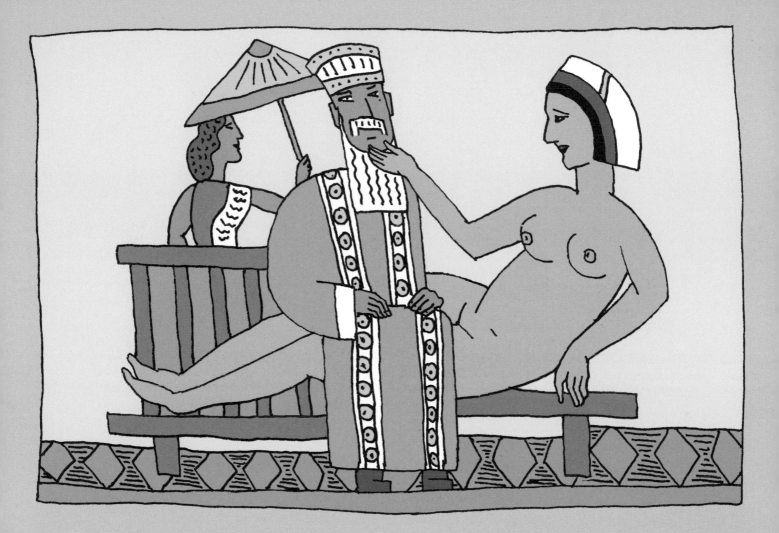

Inanna's Underworld Descent

MIDDLE EAST

Inanna, the Sumerian goddess of heaven, descends into the underworld attempting to extend the reach of her rule. The eponymous Sumerian poem *The Descent of Inanna* (c. 2100–1600 BC) chronicles the journey of the goddess from her realm in the sky to earth and down into the underworld to visit her recently widowed sister Ereshkigal, queen of the dead. Inanna is dressed in her finest clothes and wears the crown of heaven on her head, beads around her neck and her breastplate with golden rings, and she carries her scepter, the rod of power. This show of glitter upsets her sister, who orders the underworld gatekeeper to bolt the doors shut. Ereshkigal contrives a scheme to have her power-craving sister remove an article of clothing in order to pass through each gate to the underworld. After seven gates, Inanna finds herself naked and powerless, standing before Ereshkigal. The seven judges of the underworld find her guilty of hubris and strike her dead.

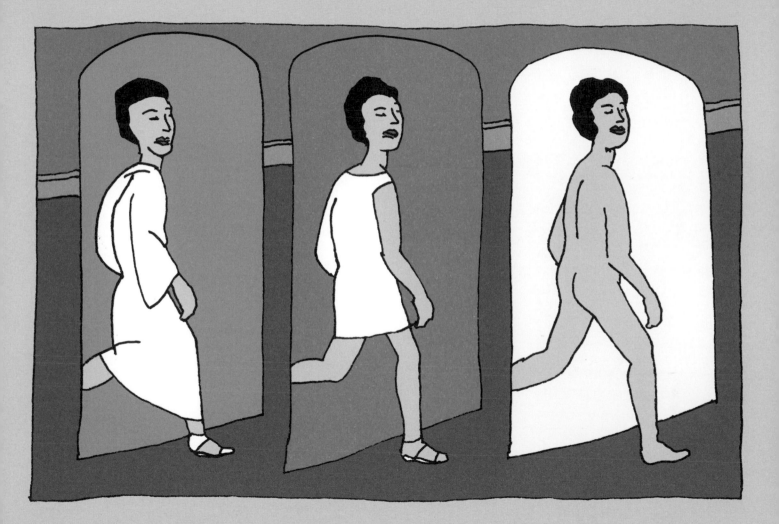

America was a promised land for many. And it promised to be a living hell for its native peoples, who ultimately endured the colonization, manifest destiny, genocide and impoverishment of the North and South American continents. With the onslaught from Europe, the white devils brought with them disease, war and slavery. The earthly hell was perhaps as torturous as the spiritual one.

XIBALBA, MAYA MYTHOLOGY

A court is held right below the surface of the earth for the twelve Lords of Xibalba, who rule over human suffering. Xibalba, or "Place of Fright," is the name of the city-like Mayan underworld, and its entrance is considered to be in front of a cave near Cobán, Guatemala, as well as nearby Belize. Xibalba is full of traps and obstacles for the dead, and when they arrive at the Xibalba council area, they are expected to greet the seated Lords. To confuse and humiliate the humans, realistic models are placed near the Lords; the disoriented humans are then invited to sit upon a seemingly innocent bench that is actually a hot cooking surface. The Lords of Xibalba amuse themselves by humiliating the people before sending them into one of Xibalba's six deadly houses, filled with even more trials that must be endured.

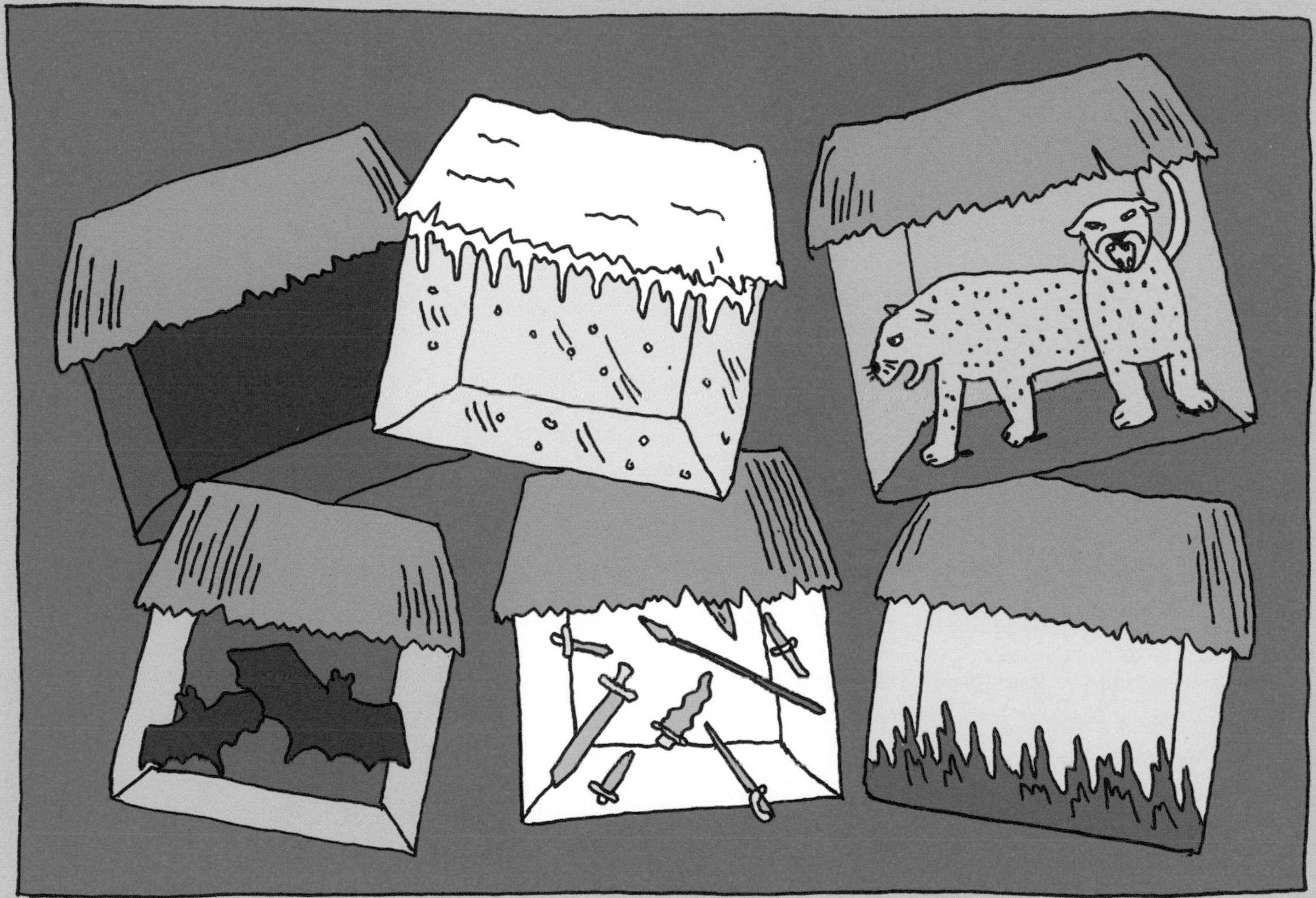

The Aztecs' Last Trip

The Aztecs were a Mesoamerican culture that flourished in central Mexico in the post-classic period from 1300 to 1521. The cosmology of Aztec religion divides the world into thirteen heavens and nine earthly layers or netherworlds. The Aztec dead are spiritually transported to Mictlan, the fearsome underworld, a gloomy, dank and starkly depressing place full of worms crawling through rotting bones. The journey takes four desperate years, and travelers have to overcome such tests as passing mountains crashing into each other, a field where the wind carries flesh-scraping knives and a river of blood filled with jaguars.

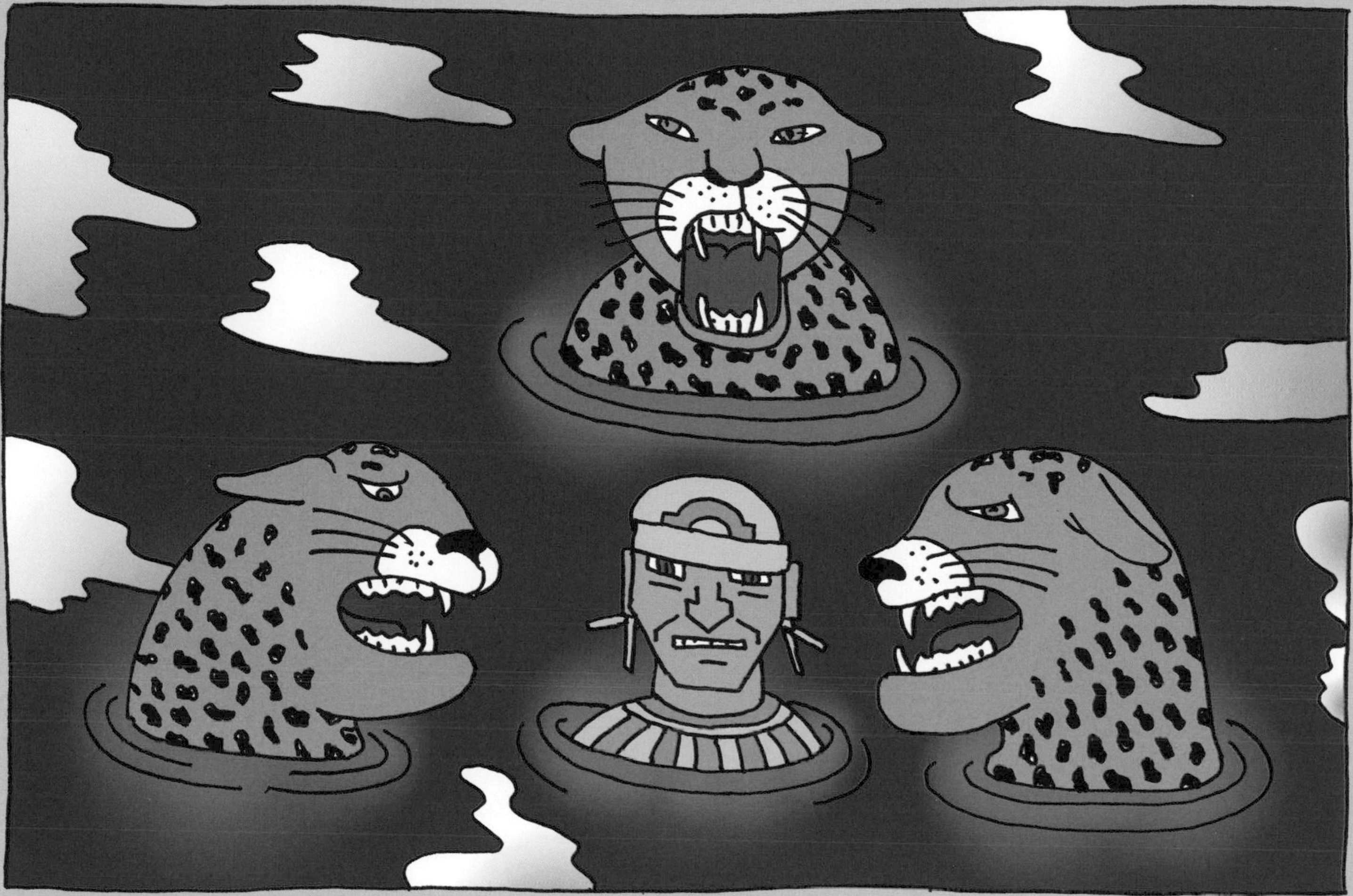

MICTLANTECUHTLI

The Aztec mythological god of the dead and the underground, whose name is Mictlantecuhtli, rules the lowest section of the underworld together with his wife Mictecacihuatl. He is a six-foot-tall, blood-splattered skeleton who wears a headdress decorated with owl feathers and a necklace made of human eyeballs. The Aztecs did not believe that the gods of the dead passed any judgment on them. One's fate in the afterlife is based only on the manner of death. Three types of souls are assigned to different parts of Mictlantechutli's domain — those who die normal deaths (of old age, diseases), heroic deaths (during battle, or sacrifice) and unheroic deaths. Each is worse than the other.

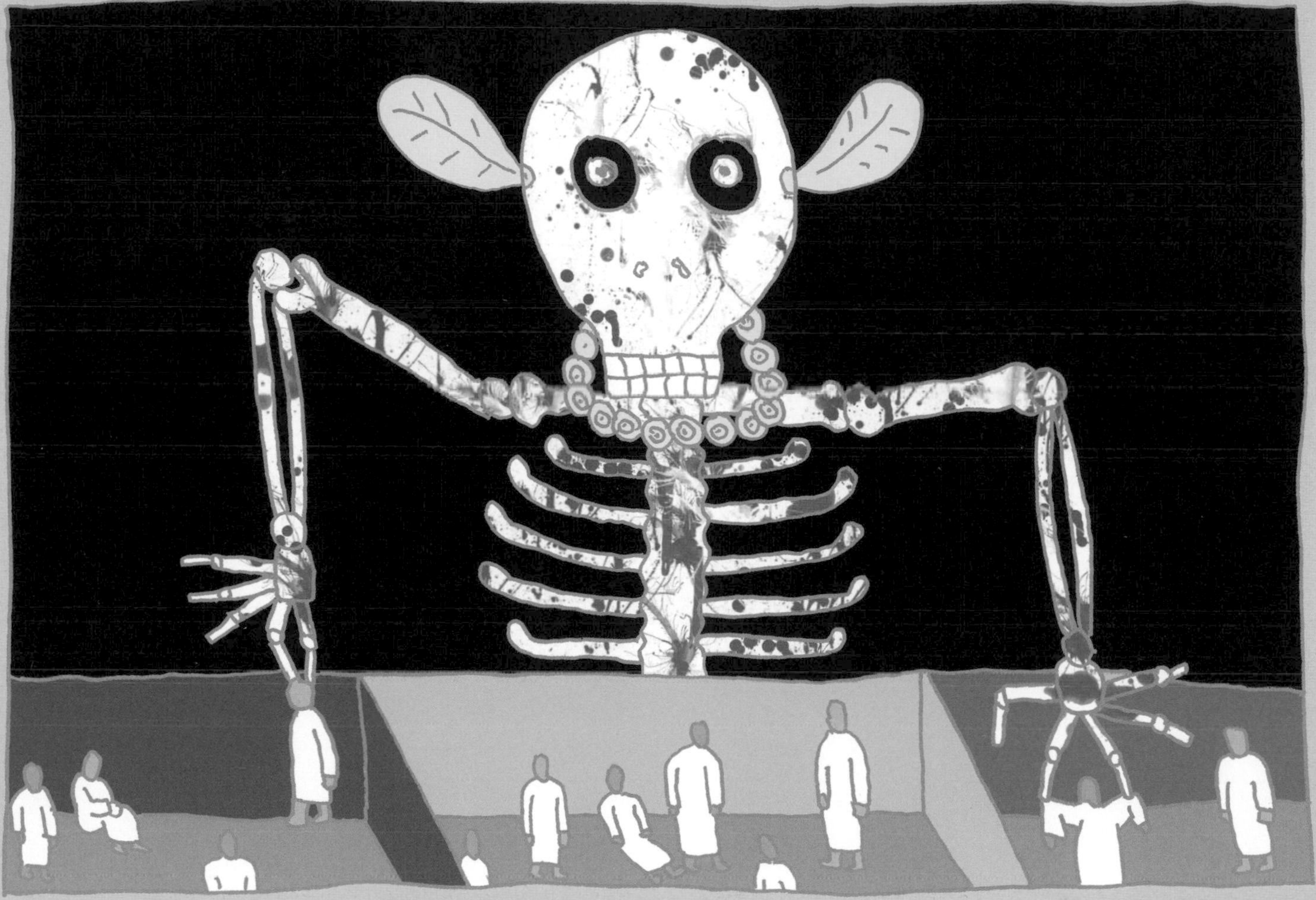

Supay, Inca God of Death

The Inca was the largest empire in South America from the fourteenth to the sixteenth century. In Inca tradition, dead evil souls are each treated to a punishing audience with Supay, the god of death. He resides in hell, inside the earth, lusting after humans who kill each other, and voraciously feeds on their souls.

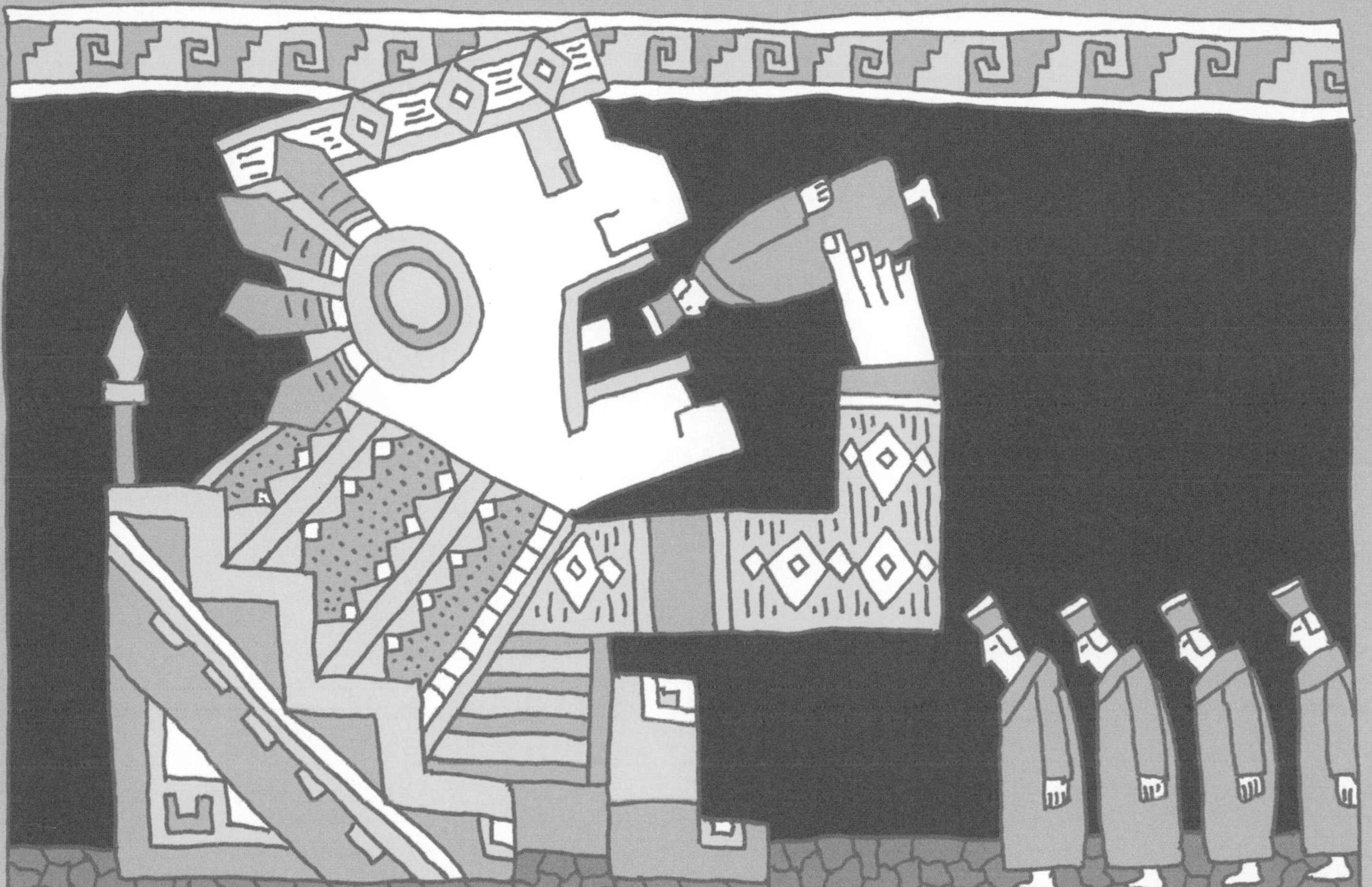

Iroquois Beliefs

A North American Iroquois tribal myth invokes Hahgwehdaetgah as father of evil who rules the burning underworld. The Iroquois believe that his kingdom is located below the earth and filled with broken bodies of enemies. Like in other cultures, Hahgwehdaetgah has a twin brother, Hahgwehdiyu, the good god. Hahgwehdaetgah killed their mother in childbirth, then he created all that was vile on earth and was thus exiled below. The two brothers fought, and Hahgwehdaetgah was defeated by the good Hahgwehdiyu with an enchanted arrow. Hahgwehdaetgah remained as overlord of the dead and oversaw the demons who terrorize earth.

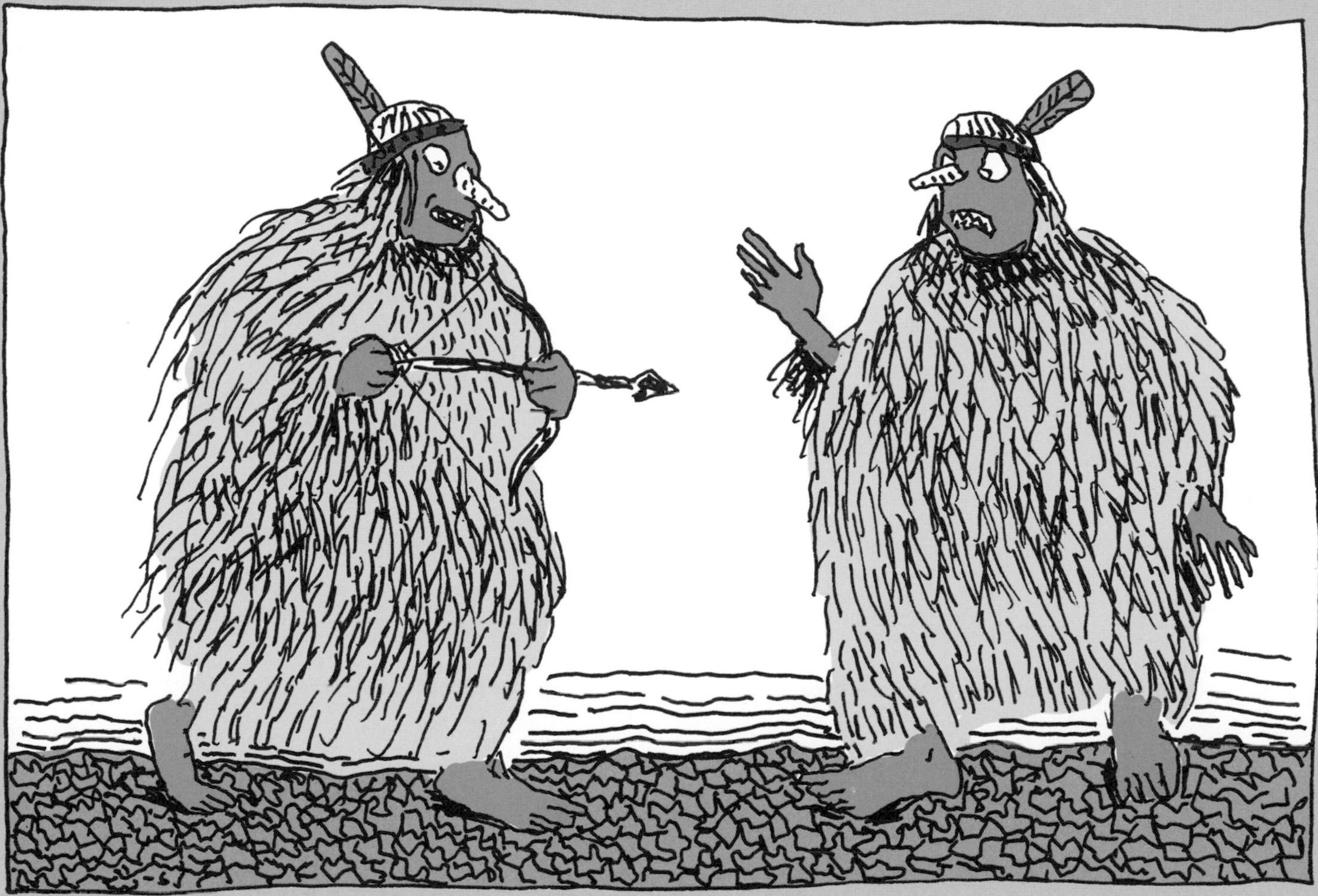

GHEDE

In Haiti, the family of Ghede represents the powers of death and fertility. Papa Ghede, lord of death, is the corpse of the first human who ever died. He is curiously conceived as a short man, dressed in a black dinner jacket and always with a top hat and sunglasses. He is known to smoke cheap cigars and eat apples. He guides souls into the afterlife yet has a soft spot for children, refusing to take anyone before their time. He swears to protect all little ones. He also has the power to resurrect the dead and to bring zombies back to life.

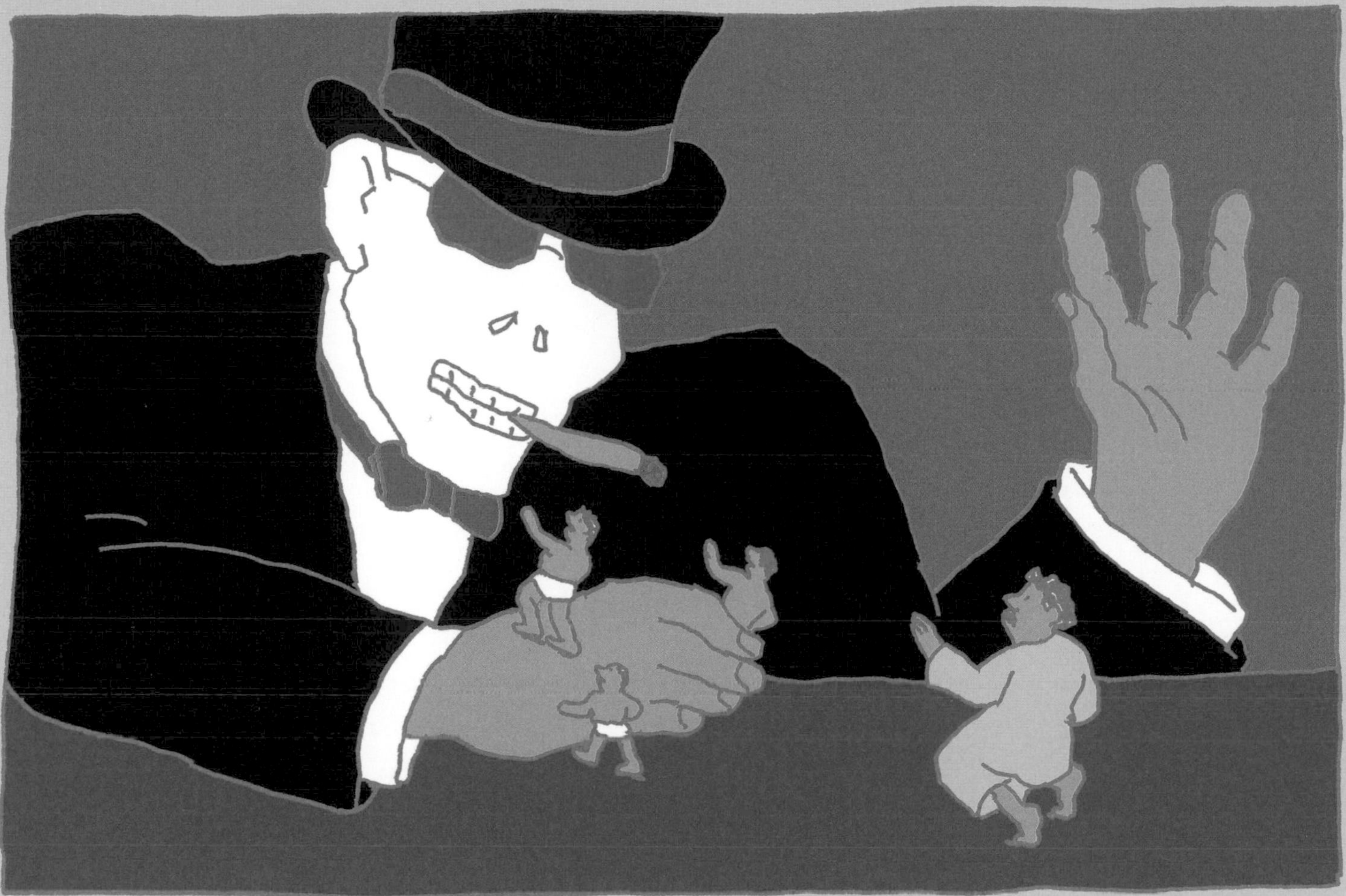

frican tradition that has not been transformed through Christian teaching includes a benign afterlife where ancestors spend their eternity. Most Africans do not fear a hereafter where entry is based on behavior or morality during earthly existence. There is nothing to attain and less to fear; there is no paradise or anguish, no reward or retribution. In essence, African peoples believe in a God that judges and punishes those who transgress during their earthly state, but not after death. There are, however, a few exceptions where evildoers are punished by ancestors after death—they go to a place that's eternally cold, while good people are drawn to everlasting light.

Swahili Hell

In African Swahili belief, hell is a deep icy abyss into which the damned are thrown. Hell in Swahili is also known as Jehanum. It has seven levels. The lowest level is for the worst of the worst sinners; it is perpetual and unending coldness. The seventh level is reserved for ultimate evil; yet other rings are defined by degrees. The sixth level, for instance, offers possible salvation —but don't hold your breath, it could take millennia.

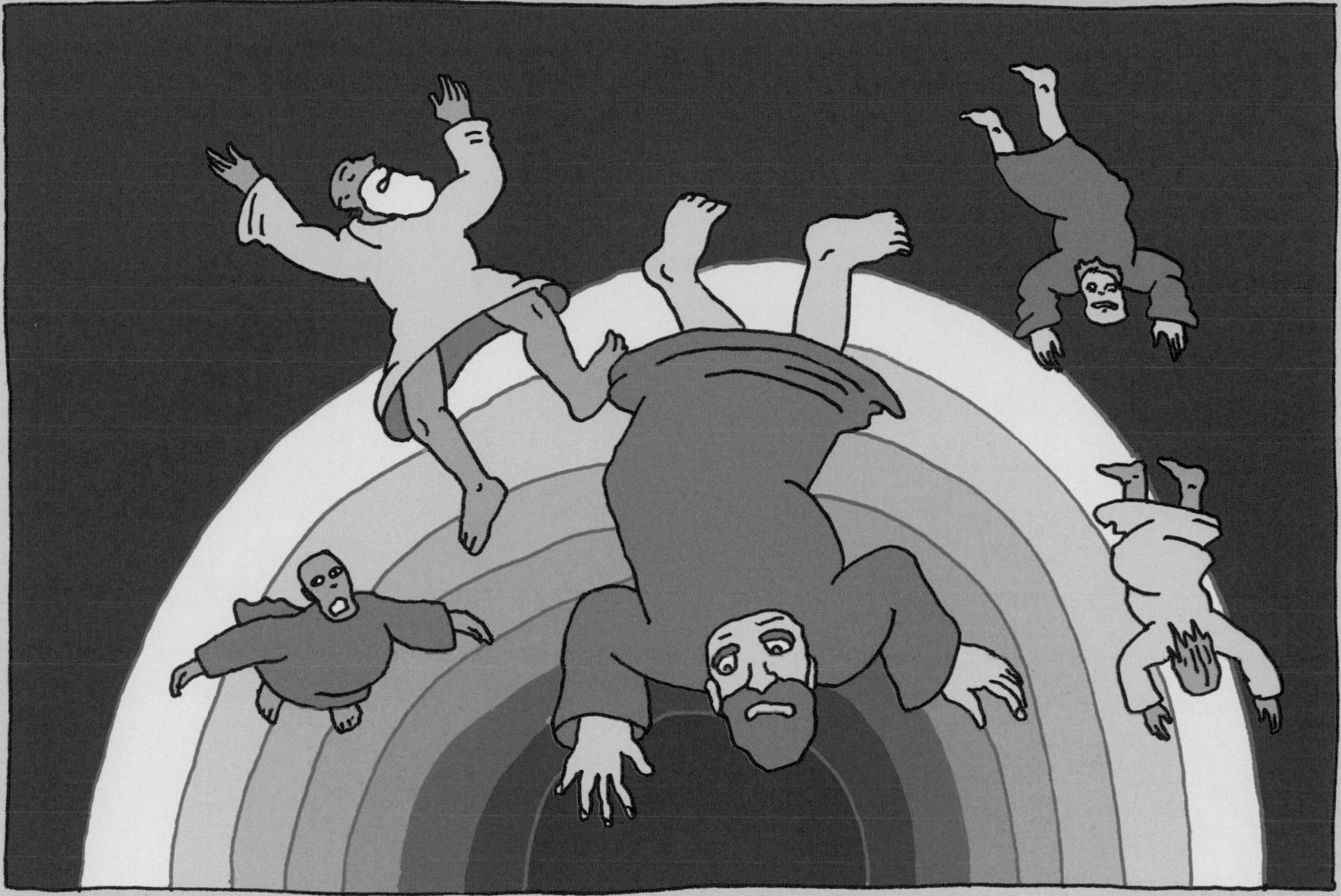

Koisan Mythology

Ga-Gorib, according to a myth from South Africa, is a leopard-like monster who would trick people into throwing stones in a bottomless pit. The stones always rebound and hit the one who threw them, who would thus fall into the pit to spend the rest of eternity in the horrid ground. Ga-Gorib's cohort, Heitsi-Eibib, has the power to return from the grave and renounce his sins.

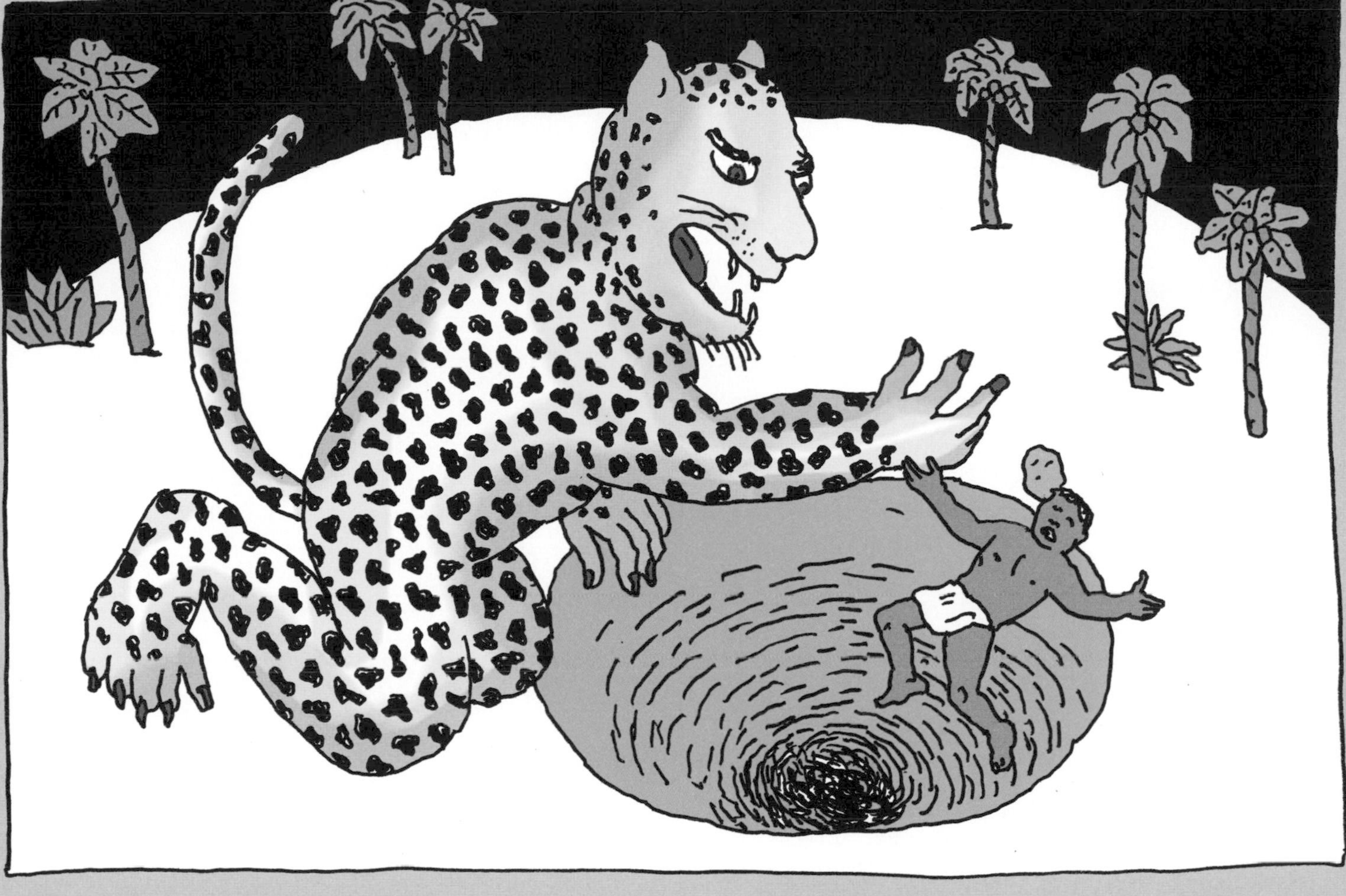

KING KITAMBA OF ANGOLA

Upset at the sudden death of his bride, Queen Muhongo, King Kitamba mourns her for days, not eating, drinking or speaking. He sends a shaman to the underworld to bring her back to life. The shaman digs a hole in his hut and reaches the dull, dank area of the underworld, called Kalunga. Queen Muhongo is denied return to the land of the living by the Lord Kalunga-ngombe, king of the netherworld. Instead, King Kitamba looks forward to his own death to be united with his wife.

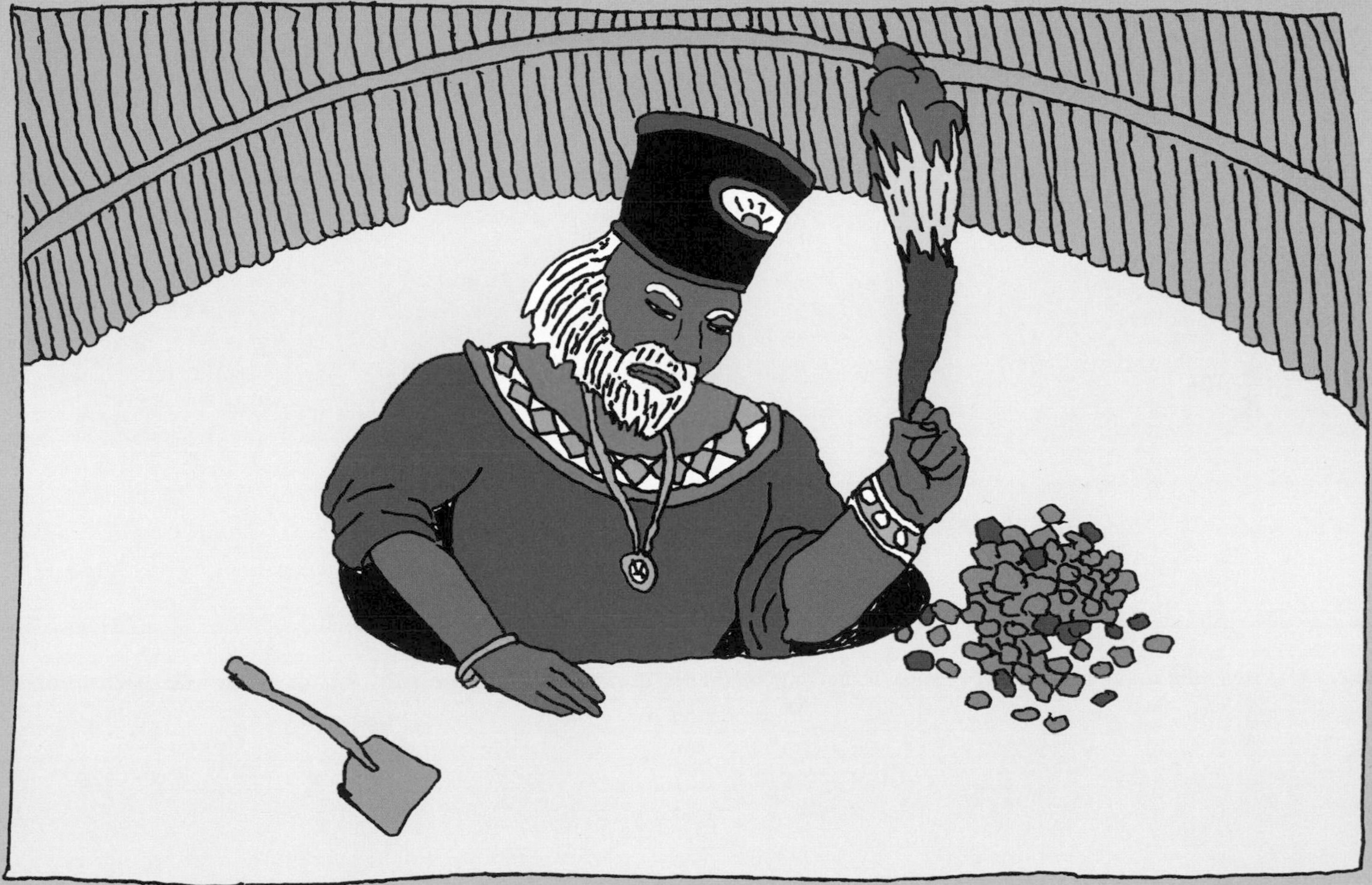

Egyptian Book of the Dead

Early Egyptians believed in judgment after death. The deceased might encounter lakes of fire, crocodiles, snakes and locusts. The *Book of the Dead* was a collection of magic spells intended to guide a soul's journey through the Duat, or the underworld, and was placed in sarcophagi with the deceased starting around 1550 BC. Priests added texts for over a thousand years. The *Book* is divided into chambers, each containing a variety of horrors souls must know the correct magic spells for; if they don't, they will be either devoured by serpents or tortured and forced to eat human excrement—sometimes all three. If they manage to pass these trials they can face the Weighing of the Heart test.

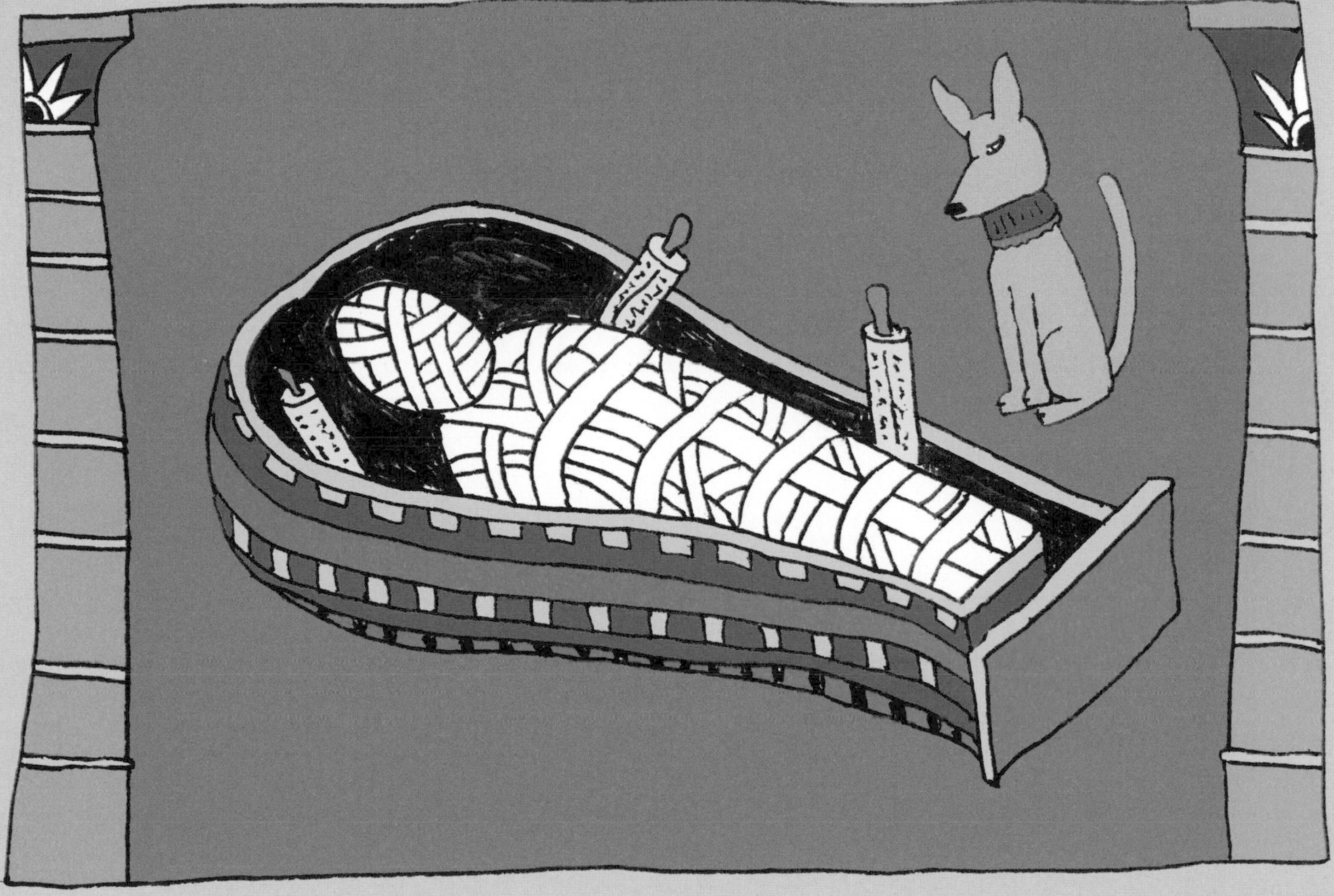

Egyptian Book of the Dead II

A deceased person travels in a boat with others to Duat. After successfully passing various horrors and trials, they reach the Hall of Justice, where King Osiris asks for an account of good and evil acts. Every soul's heart is weighed on a scale against the feather of Ma'at, the goddess of truth. If the heart is lighter than the feather, the soul is allowed to pass into the afterlife. If not, a beast known as Ammit, the Devourer of the Dead (composed of lion, crocodile and hippopotamus), swallows the heart, and the soul becomes eternally restless.

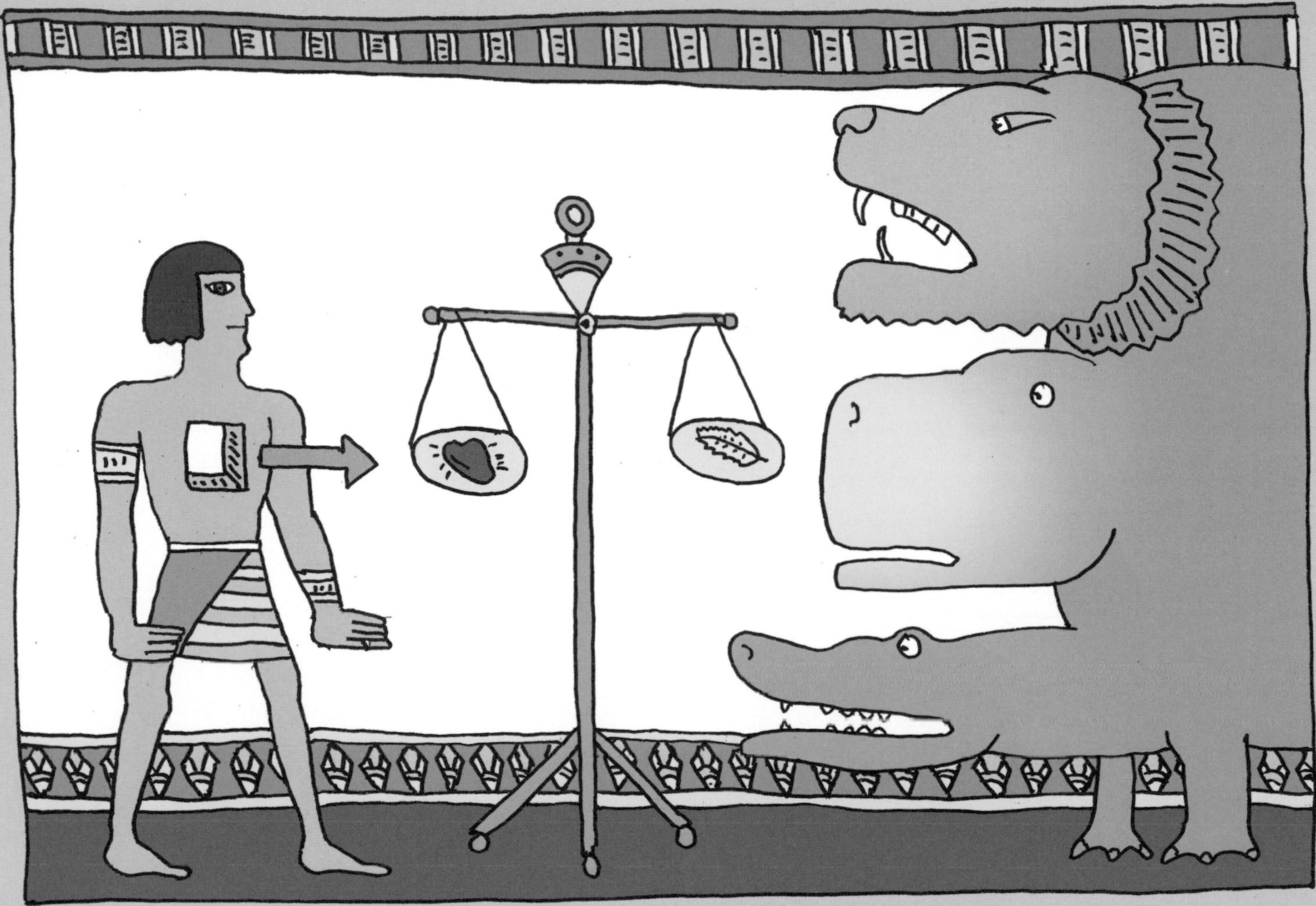

ades derives from Greek mythology and refers to the god of the underworld; it is also the home of the dead, where all people go when they die. In Matthew 16:18, Jesus takes this word and applies his own specific, though limited, descriptions to it. "Hades" is not as widely used as "hell," and it doesn't carry the unbiblical connotations for most people. More horrifying is the Lake of Fire, mentioned in *Revelation* 19:20 and 20:10, 14–15, the final place of eternal punishment for all unrepentant rebels, both angelic and human (Matthew 25:41).

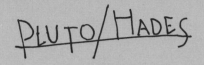

PLUTO/HADES

In Greek mythology, Pluto is the son of the Titan Cronus and brother of Poseidon and Zeus. After defeating the Titans in war, the brothers divide between themselves the realms to rule: Zeus receives the sky, Poseidon the seas, and Pluto becomes the ruler of the underworld. The earlier name for the god was Hades, which became more common as the name of the underworld itself. Persephone is Pluto's consort and the queen of the underworld. She is promised to him by Zeus, her father, but she does not go willingly: she is abducted by Hades and kept prisoner in the underworld. Desperate for her return, her mother Demeter, goddess of the harvest, decides that the earth will remain barren until she sees her daughter again. At the end a compromise is reached: Persephone will only spend one-third of the year in the underworld, during which winter falls upon the earth.

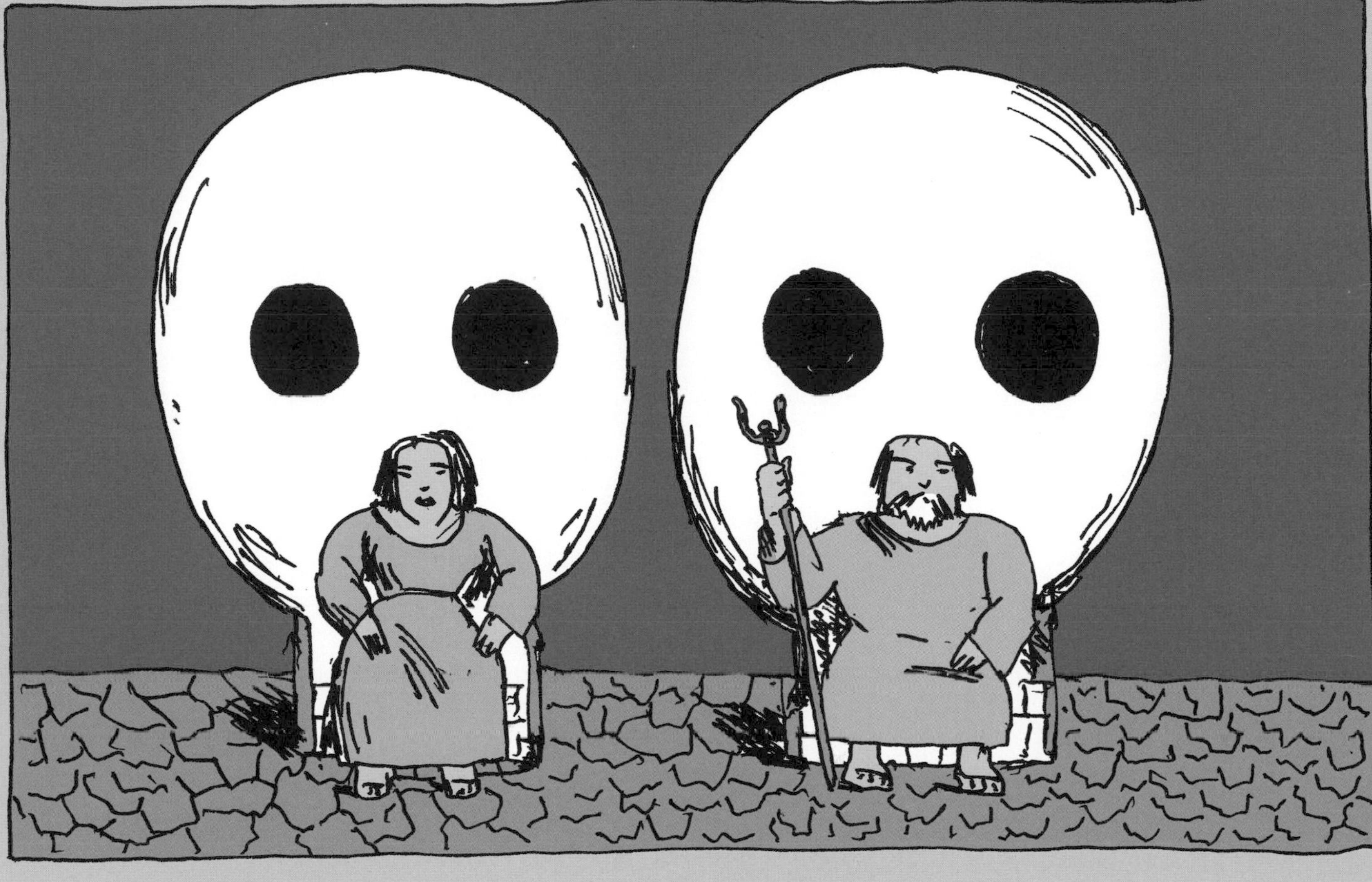

Sisyphus

In Greek mythology, Sisyphus is known as a crafty trickster who tried twice to cheat death. He betrays Zeus by revealing the whereabouts of Aegina, whom Zeus wrongfully kidnapped for himself, to her father. Angry, Zeus punishes Sisyphus by ordering Thanatos (Death) to chain Sisyphus in Tartarus, the lowest part of the underworld. Sisyphus asks Thanatos for a demonstration of the chain but Thanatos chains himself. With that, no one could die on earth. General Ares is annoyed since Sisyphus had taken away the pleasure of seeing the enemy soldiers die, so he frees Thanatos and Sisyphus is taken to Tartarus. After his death, though, he tricks Persephone to send him back to the upper world and refuses to return to the underworld, until Hermes drags him back. Furious at Sisyphus and his hubris, Zeus punishes Sisyphus by having him push a giant boulder up a hill. But just as clever, Zeus enchants the boulder to roll back down before it reaches the top, leaving Sisyphus to repeat the futile task for eternity.

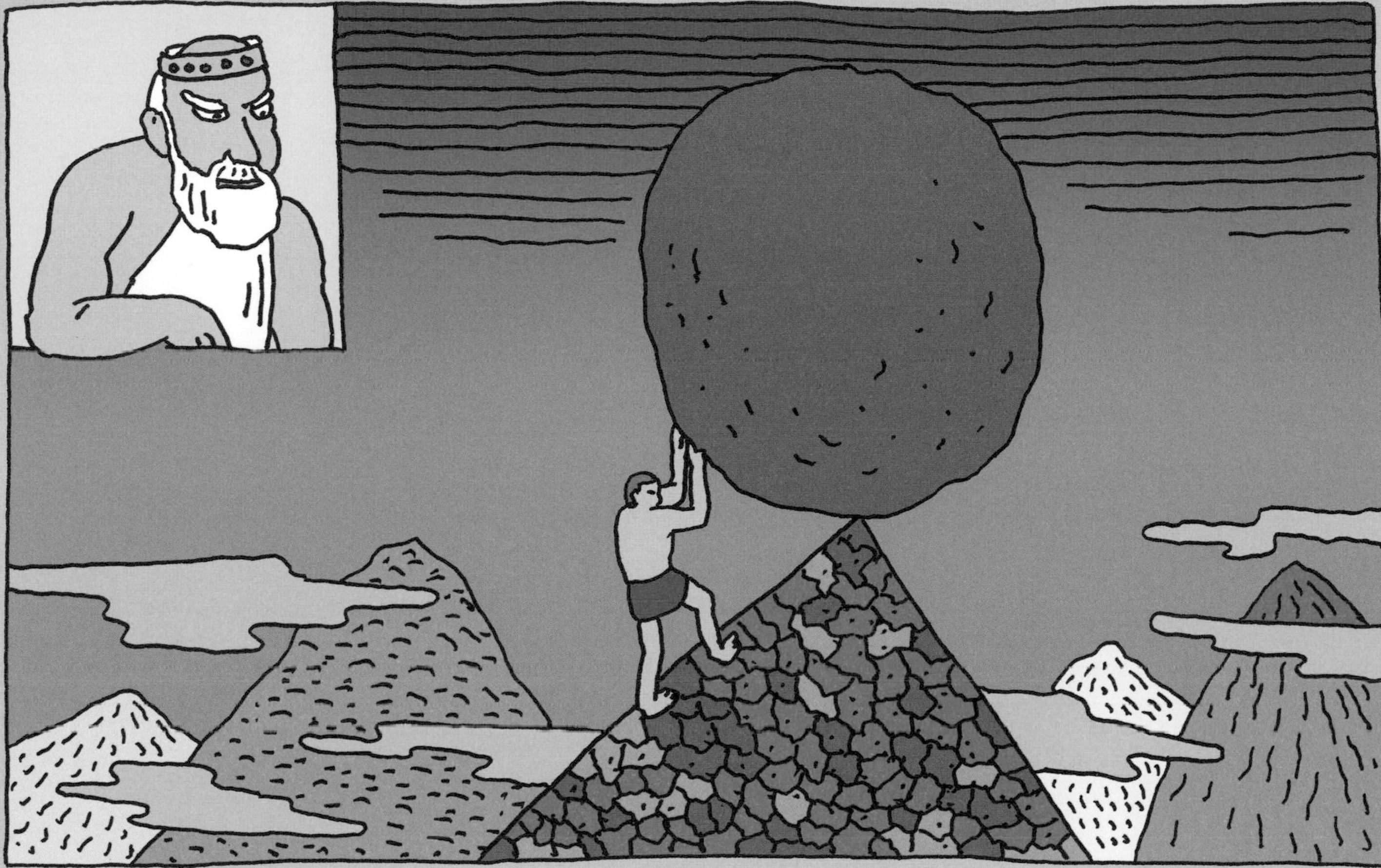

HERCULES

Son of Zeus and a mortal woman, Hercules is known
in Greek mythology for his extraordinary strength.
He descends to Hades to capture Cerberus as the last of the
twelve labors he is forced to perform to become immortal.
Cerberus is a doglike monster with three heads, who
guards the entrance of hell. This labor is deemed impossible
to perform but Hercules convinces Hades to grant him
permission to take the hound.

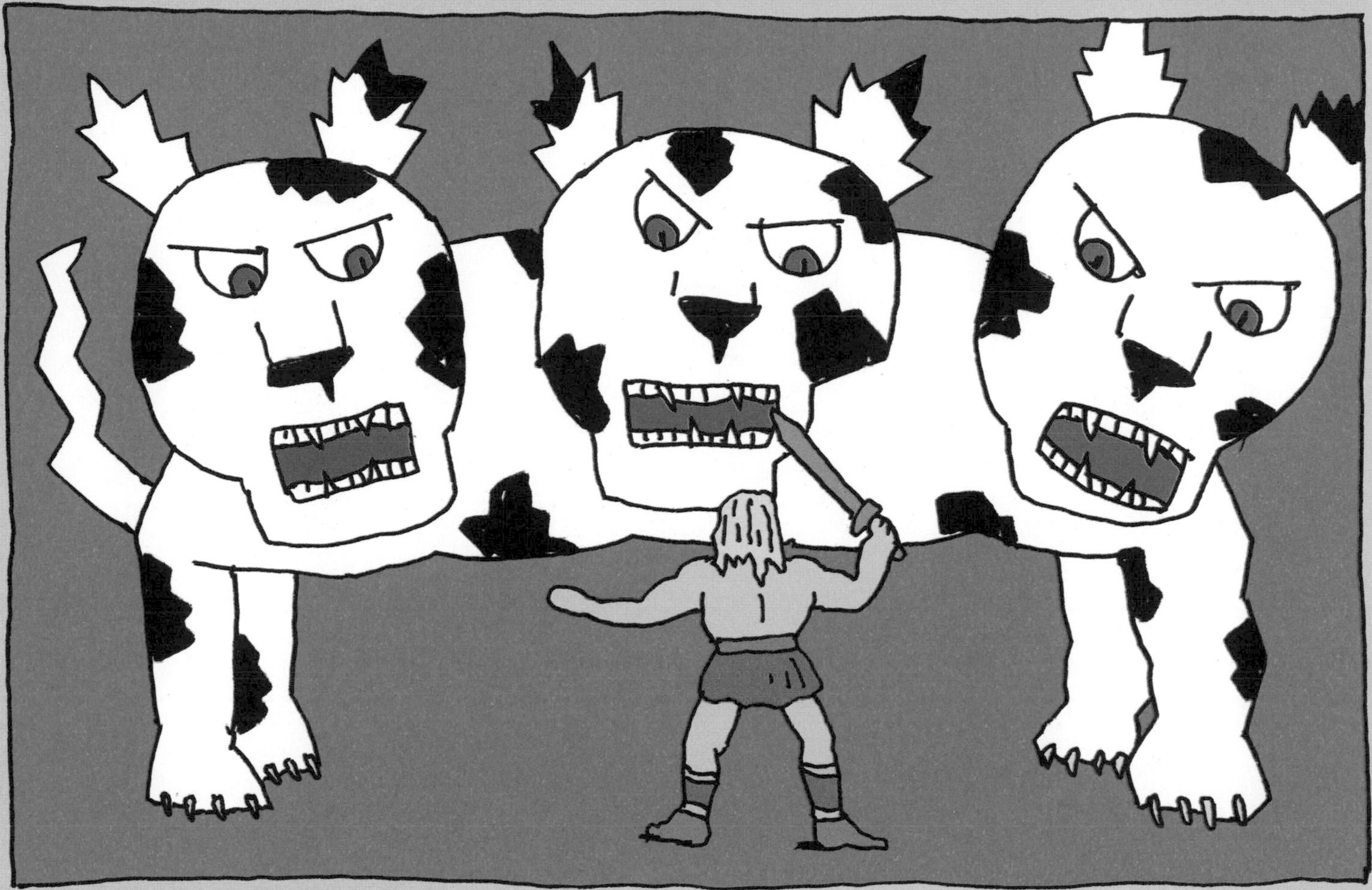

DANAIDES' PUNISHMENT

GREECE

The Danaides are the fifty daughters of Danaus, who are forced to marry fifty brothers, sons of Aegyptus, Danaus's twin brother. All but one of the daughters kill their husbands on their wedding night and for punishment are condemned to spend eternity in Hades, where they are forced to carry water in a sieve with holes. Hypermnestra is the only one who doesn't kill her husband, because he respects her desire to remain a virgin. Her husband, Lynceus, later kills Danaus as revenge for the murder of his brothers.

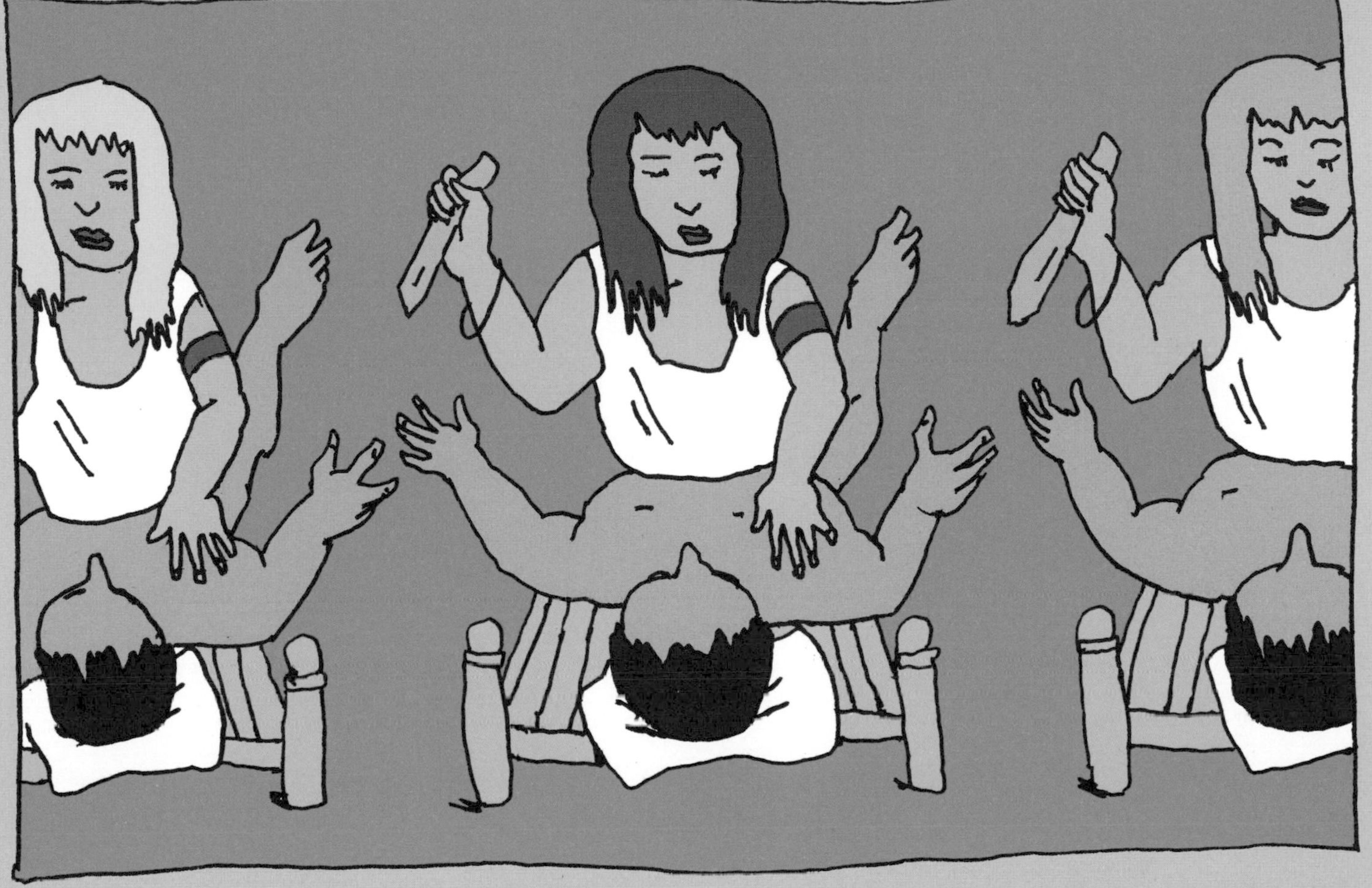

SOCRATES AND THE WICKED

In Plato's dialogue *Phaedo*, Socrates talks about the immortality of the soul. He describes the soul as a winged creature. The perfect soul flies upward while the imperfect one droops and settles to the ground and takes on a mortal body. Wicked souls must be imprisoned in other bodies, each according to the nature of the life previously held: a drunkard in a donkey's body, a thug in a wolf's body. Those that have committed terrible crimes are thrown into Tartarus to be there forever. In Greek mythology, Tartarus is both a deity and a place in the underground.

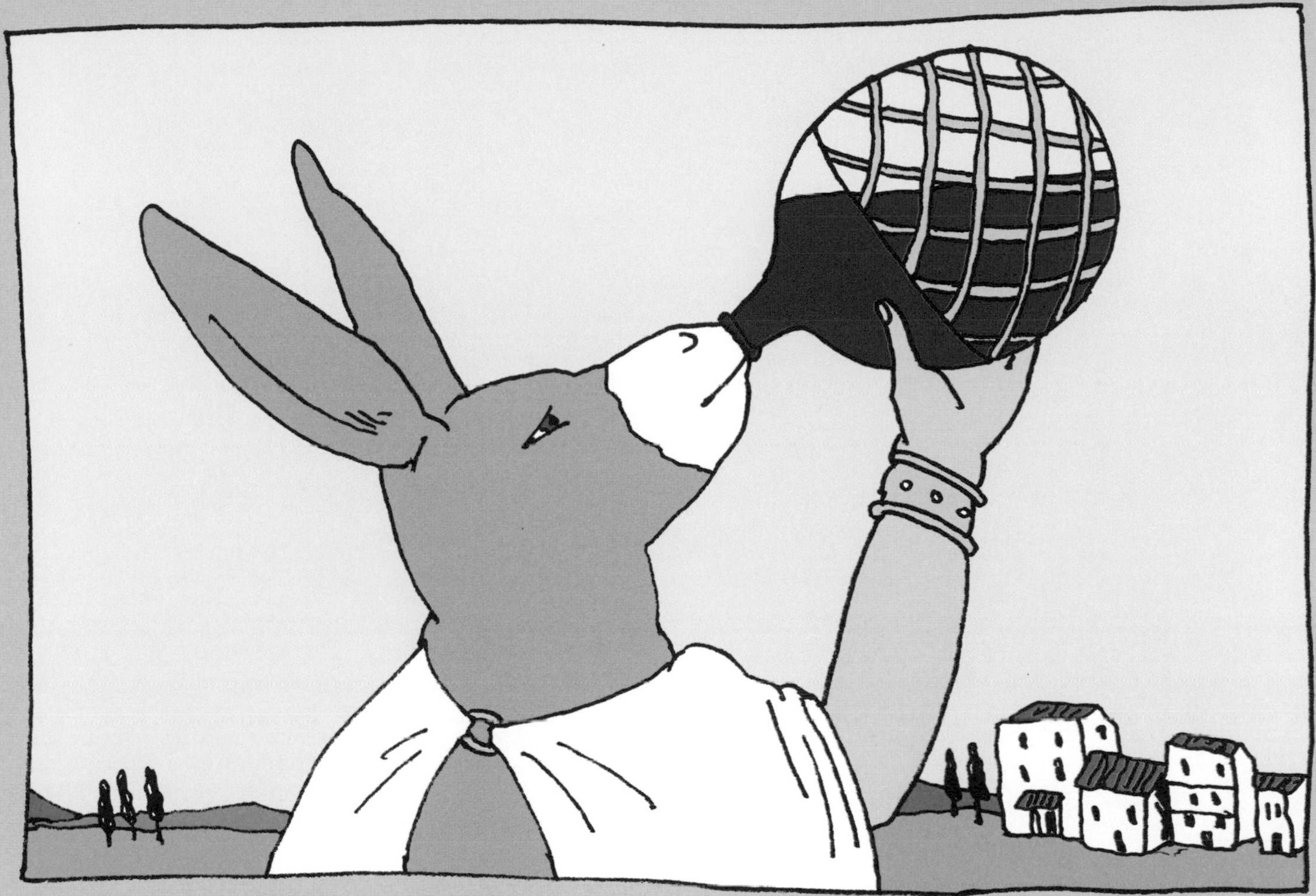

Plato's Myth of Er

In *The Republic*, Plato tells the story of Er, a soldier who was left for dead on the battlefield before reviving on his pyre. The philosopher tells of his journey through the afterlife: he comes to a place where the souls are judged, and virtuous souls ascend to heaven on the right while sinners descend on the left. Those who have committed the worst crimes are met by "wild men" who drag them off to hell and flay them with "scourges and thorns." The judges tell Er that he has to watch and report back what he sees. The souls, after having completed their time there, have then to choose their next life: those who have been punished often made a better choice than those who have ascended to the sky. Souls drink the waters of Lethe (which means "forgetfulness") and rise to be born again. Er doesn't drink and wakes up remembering everything.

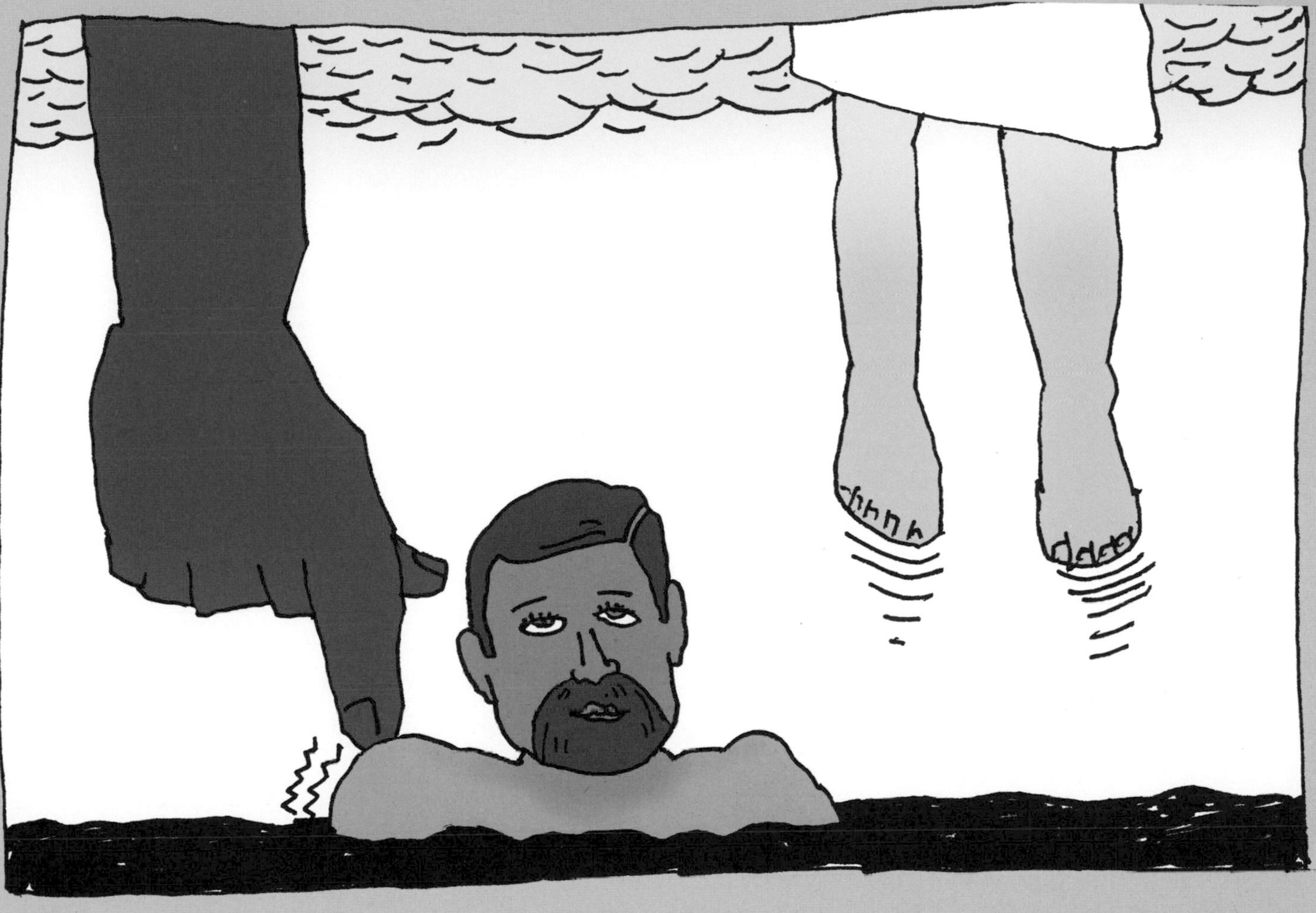

**H**ell on earth certainly influenced the common perception of hell below. The crucifix, originally a symbol of hell, was transformed into a Christian symbol representing the martyrdom of Christ. Yet he was not the first to suffer such a torturous execution. Following the final battle between the rebel slave leader Spartacus and Marcus Licinius Crassus, in 71 BC, thousands were crucified and following their torment were left to rot on crosses until their flesh melted away and their innards were picked clean by animals; flies buzzed around the rotting corpses hanging on crosses of wood in rows along the side of Appian Way leading in and out of Rome. Hell was on full view, for all to see.

LAKE AVERNUS

Lake Avernus, a volcanic crater located west of Naples, Italy, was believed to hold the entrance to the underworld, where all dead souls dwell, by ancient Greeks and Romans. It became an important place of ancient ritual and is famed for inspiring mythology. Its poisonous sulfurous vapors probably gave origin to the legend that birds that fly overhead fall dead from the sky. Lake Avernus is also featured in Virgil's *Aeneid*: the poet describes Aeneas's descent into the underworld, which recalls the journey of Odysseus in the land of the dead, as told by Homer.

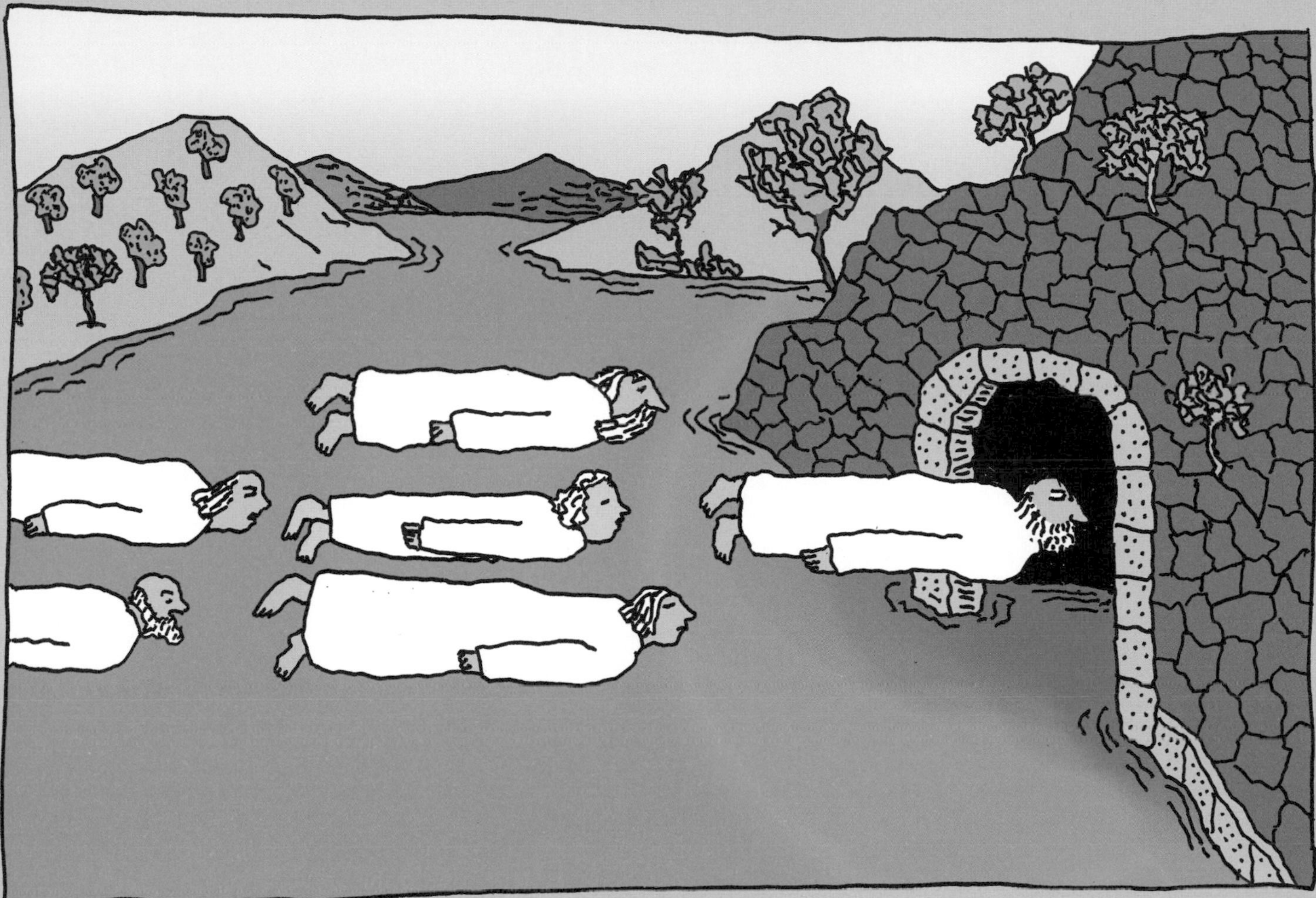

NIFLHEIM

In ancient Norse mythology, hell, called Niflheim, is not hot but icy cold with primordial darkness. It is ruled by a hideous goddess, Hel, who overlooks this wasteland of ice where the damned cry out in eternal agony. Another realm is Muspelheim, the land of fire. Both realms of fire and ice were instrumental in creating the earth: when the ice from Niflheim met the flames from Muspelheim, creation began and the first man was formed.

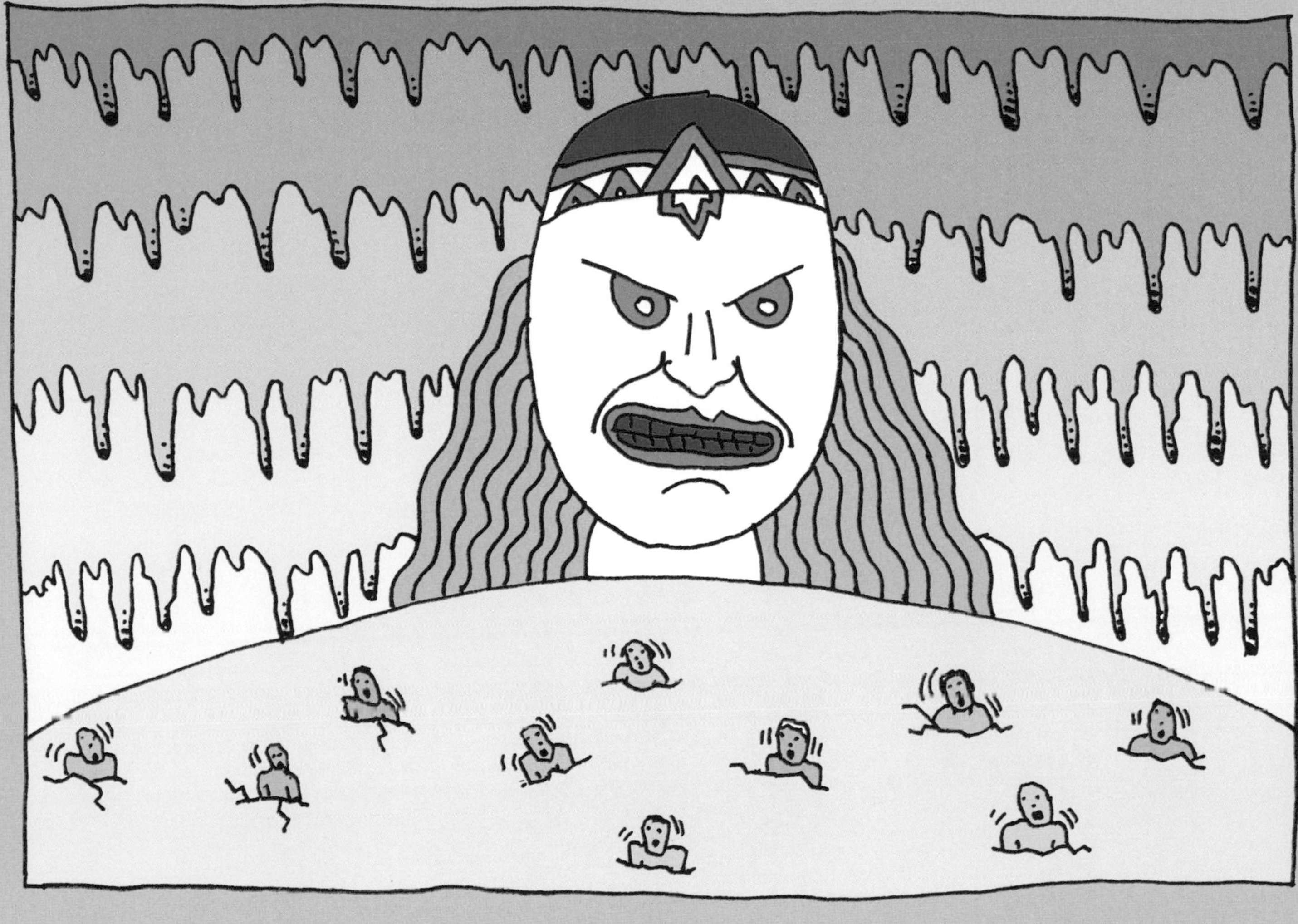

MANALA: FINNISH MYTHOLOGY

Manala is the land of the dead under the earth, according to Finno-Ugric mythology. Souls must cross a fiery stream, guarded by a black swan, to reach a dark, gloomy place but not a place of everlasting torment as in Christian hell, as the fate of good and bad people is the same. The realm of the dead is also pictured as a place where the dead are buried. Manala is found in various forms in the underworld, also to the north and the outer edges of the universe. Manala is ruled by a goddess, Louhi, a fierce hag of a creature.

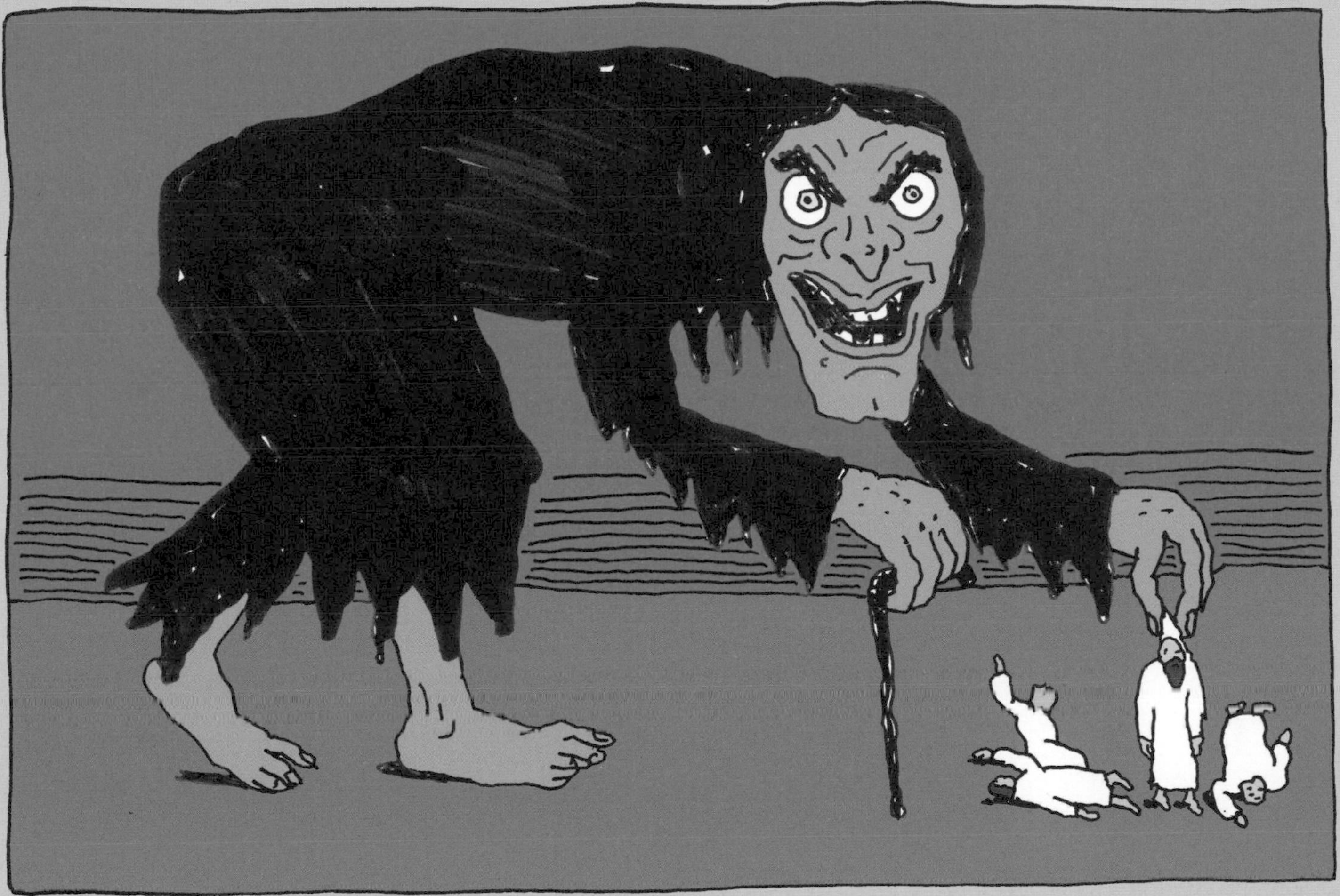

Irish Mythology

The Fomorii are a supernatural race of deformed creatures, personifying the destructive power of nature: chaos, darkness, death, blight and drought. Known for terrorizing the land and often depicted with missing limbs, the Fomorii are ruled by Balor, a one-eyed, violent giant who is the god of the dead. Uncovered, Balor's eye is a source of destruction and, to keep it from releasing its terrible power, is protected by seven layers. As each cover is removed, death and smoke gradually consume the landscape, and by the last cover the entire countryside would be set ablaze. The Fomorii are often described as hostile and monstrous beings who come from under the sea.

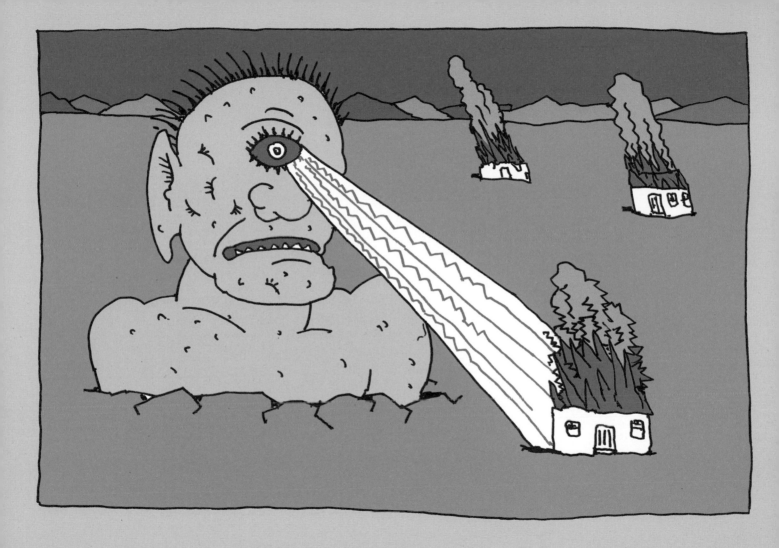

LAST JUDGMENT

God passes judgment on souls as to where their final resting place will be, whether heaven or hell. Matthew provides text for the Christian Apocalypse and Last Judgment. Jesus warns his disciples of a terrible time to come. He entreats his listeners to repent. Augustine said souls are judged when they depart from the body. Master painters, mostly from the Renaissance, have used this as a subject: Fra Angelico, Rogier van der Weyden and Michelangelo.

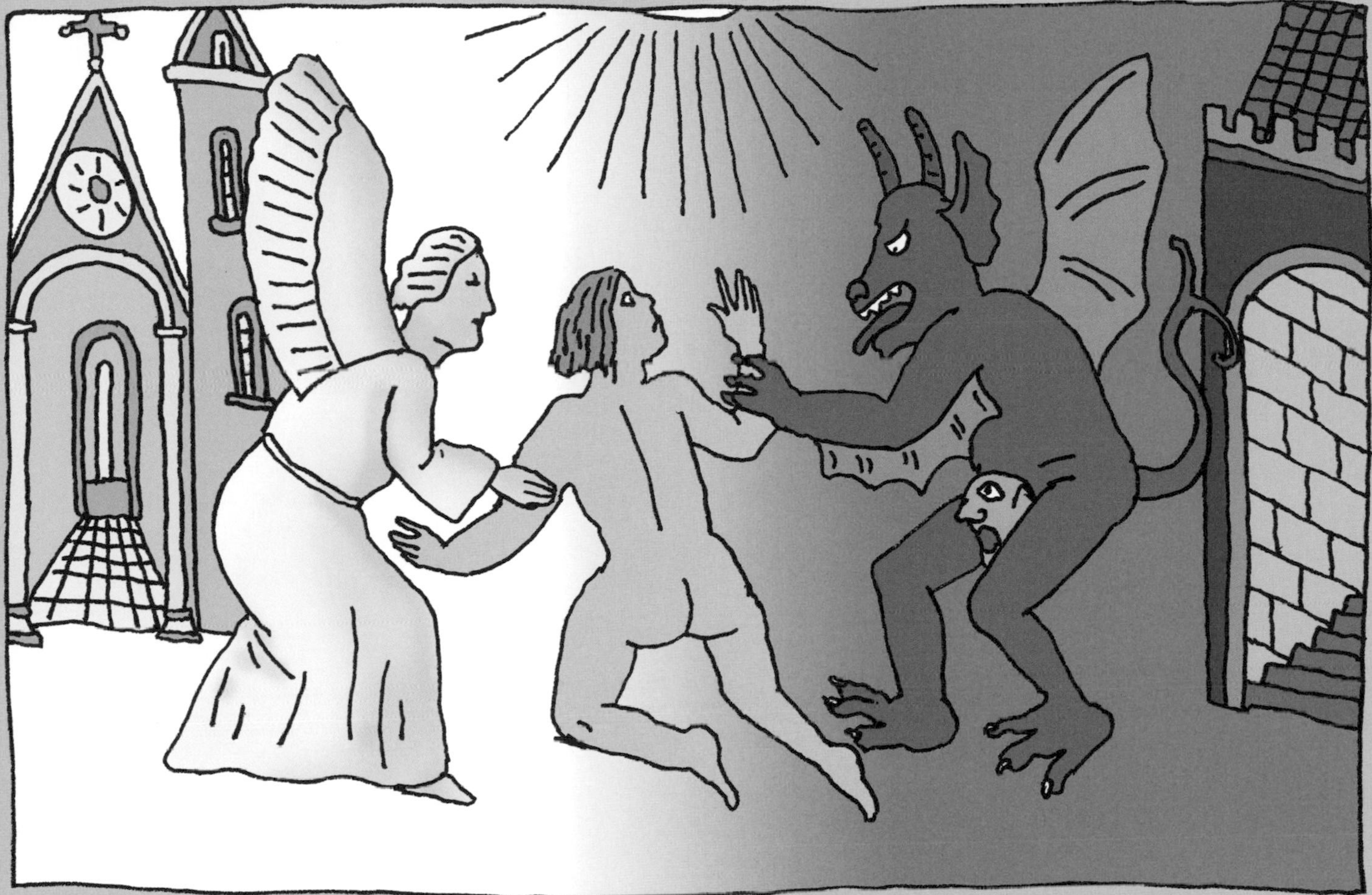

CHRISTIAN HARROWING OF HELL

EUROPE

Christ descends into hell between the time of the crucifixion and resurrection to preach to the imprisoned spirits. Adam's sin prevented anyone from entering heaven before the crucifixion, so Jesus descends into hell to free those locked-down souls. The good souls and the evil ones who promise to change their ways and convert to Christianity are redeemed.

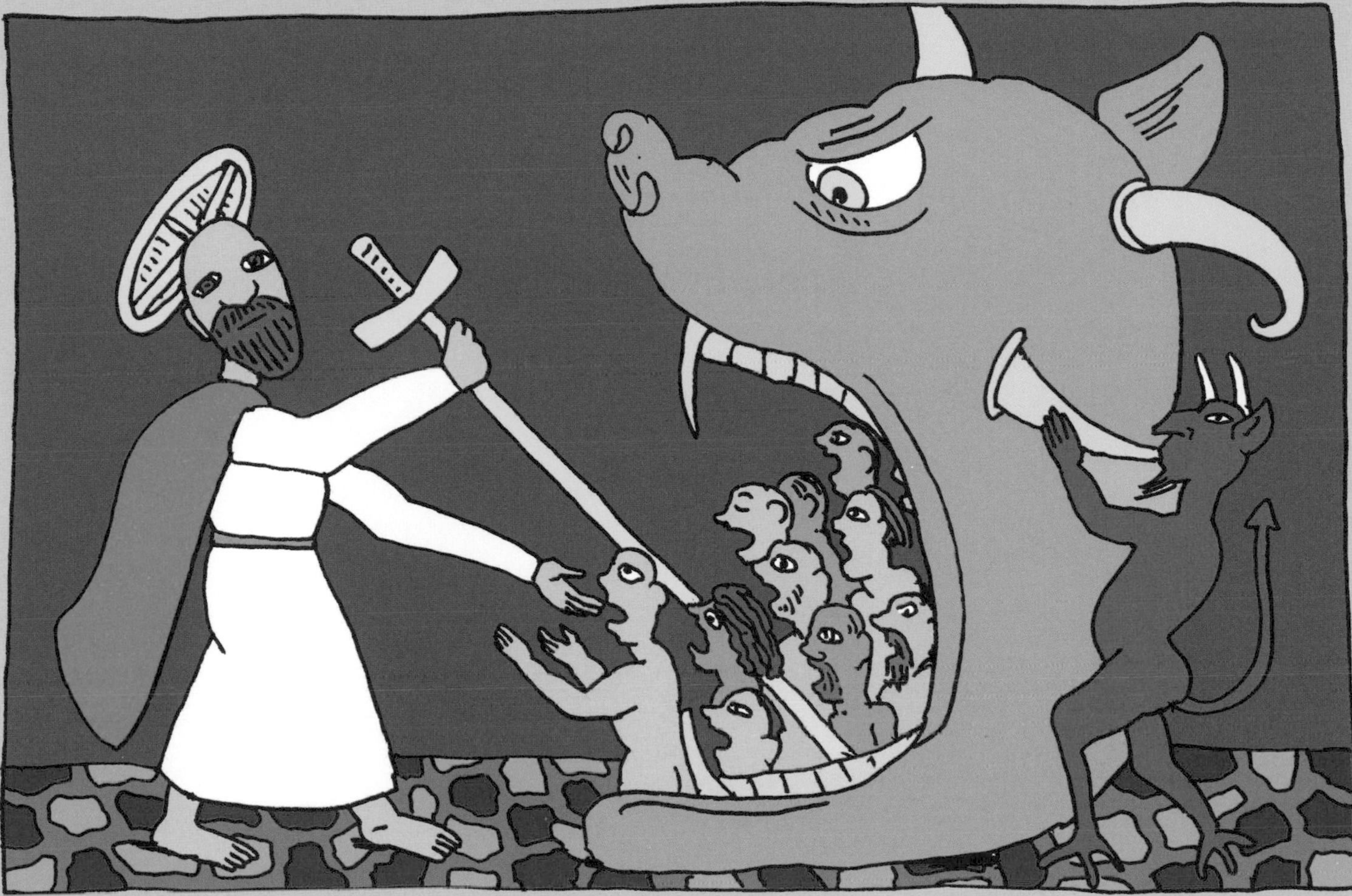

HELLMOUTH SYMBOL

The image of Hellmouth is from medieval Christianity but is found in other cultures as well. It appears in many myths and religions, including Egyptian lore, with Ammit, the Devourer of the Dead. Sometimes it is the entrance to the underworld. Other times the mouth devours sinners. It appeared in morality plays in the Middle Ages as an elaborate prop.

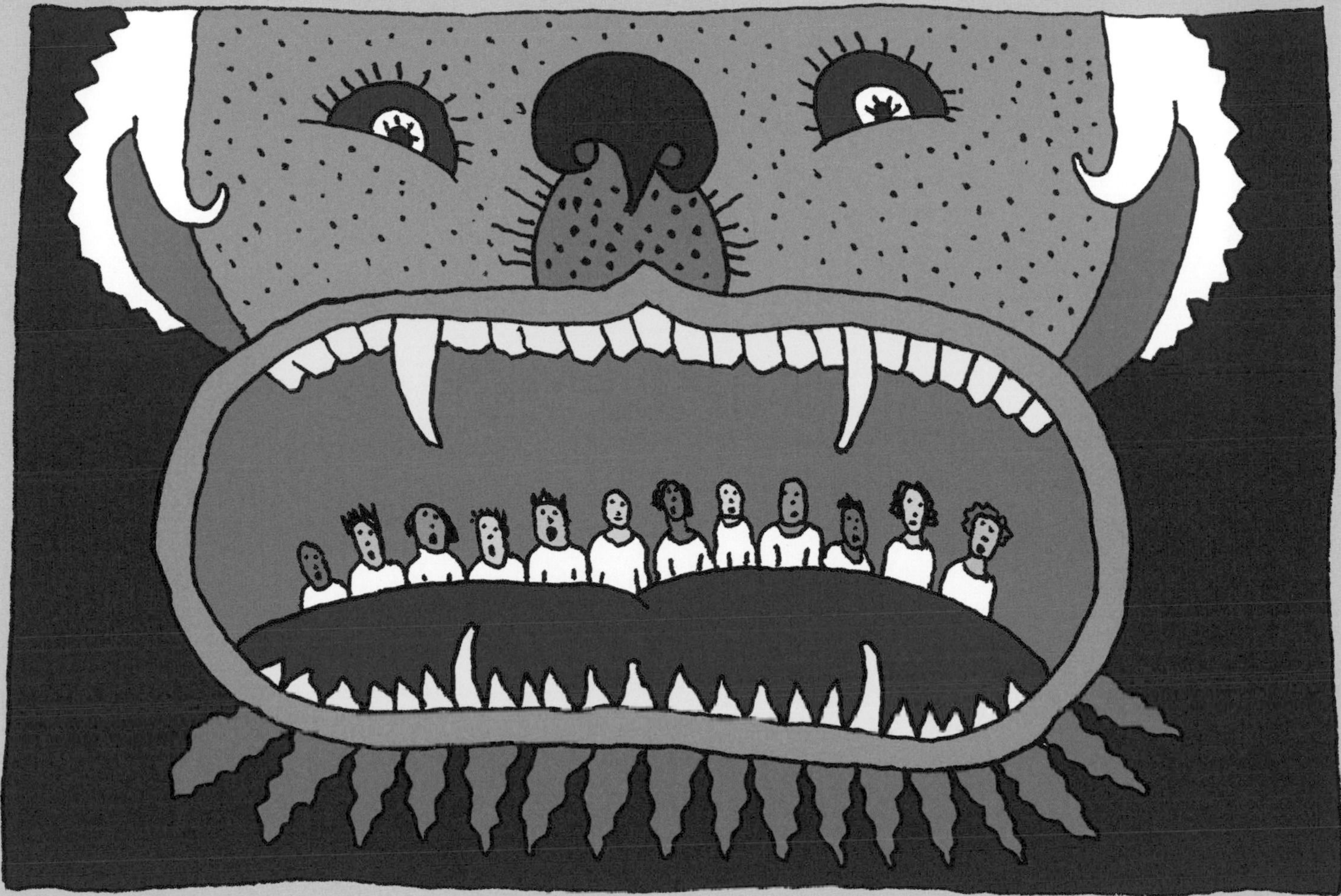

Cosmas Indicopleustes and Christian Topography

Cosmas Indicopleustes, a sixth-century merchant and traveler, offered a description of hell in his *Christian Topography* where the earth is flat, in opposition to the beliefs of most of the Christians at the time. The *Topography* is often cited as evidence that Christianity introduced the idea of the flat earth into the world. Damned souls "sleep" below the ground until the Last Judgment, when the material world will be transferred into hell.

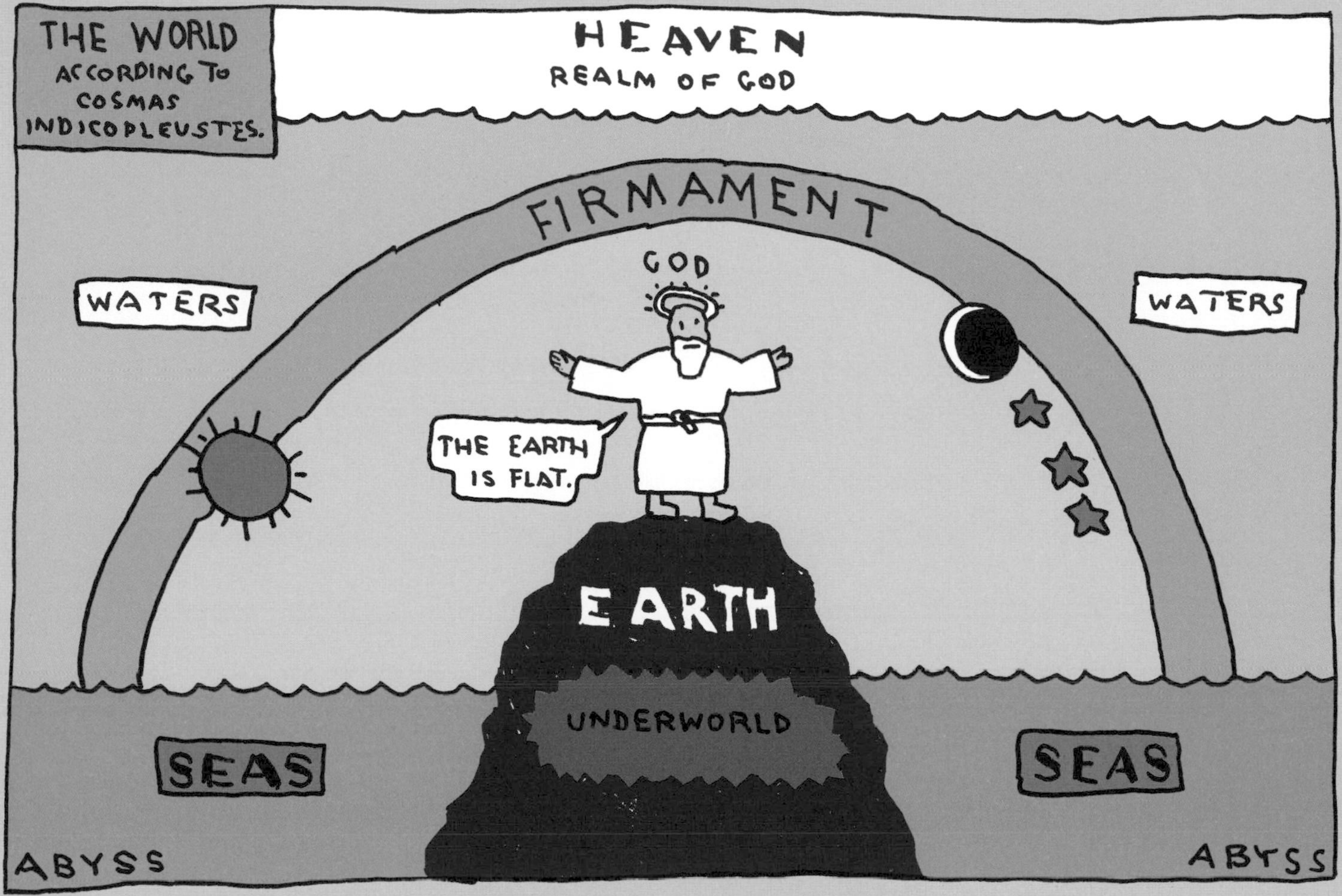
THE WORLD ACCORDING TO COSMAS INDICOPLEUSTES.
HEAVEN
REALM OF GOD
FIRMAMENT
GOD
WATERS
WATERS
THE EARTH IS FLAT.
EARTH
UNDERWORLD
SEAS
SEAS
ABYSS
ABYSS

DANTE'S HELL

The *Divine Comedy* has a detailed description of the horrors of hell. Dante is guided through the circles of the *Inferno* by the poet Virgil, who has his own view of hell in his *Aeneid*. The story was a warning to all that they have a choice of where they will spend eternity. In fact, Dante's hell is regulated by *contrapasso*, a system where punishment either resembles or contrasts with the sin itself. Deep in the eighth and penultimate circle of hell, for example, is the foul home for flatterers and frauds of language. Here, the sinners are steeped in a pit of human excrement—a typical flavor of punishment Dante would have observed.

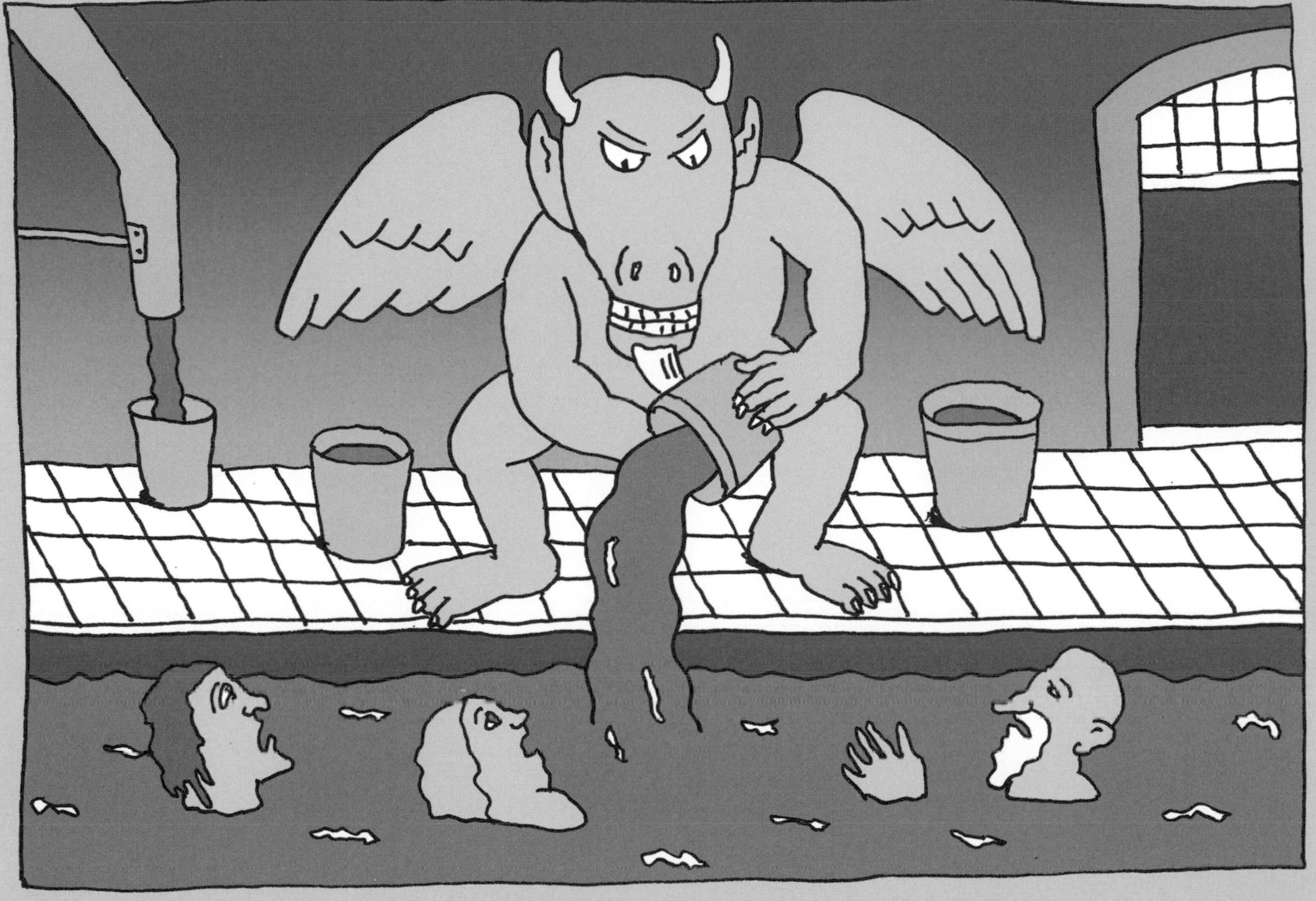

John Bunyan's Hell

The Pilgrim's Progress, written by John Bunyan in the 1600s, describes a man named Christian and his journey through hell. In a totally dark land he finds wickedly foul-smelling monsters and screaming souls regretting their sins. He encounters Apollyon, a preserver of evil, a deformed demon covered with fish scales and dragon wings. He belches smoke and stench through a hole in his body.

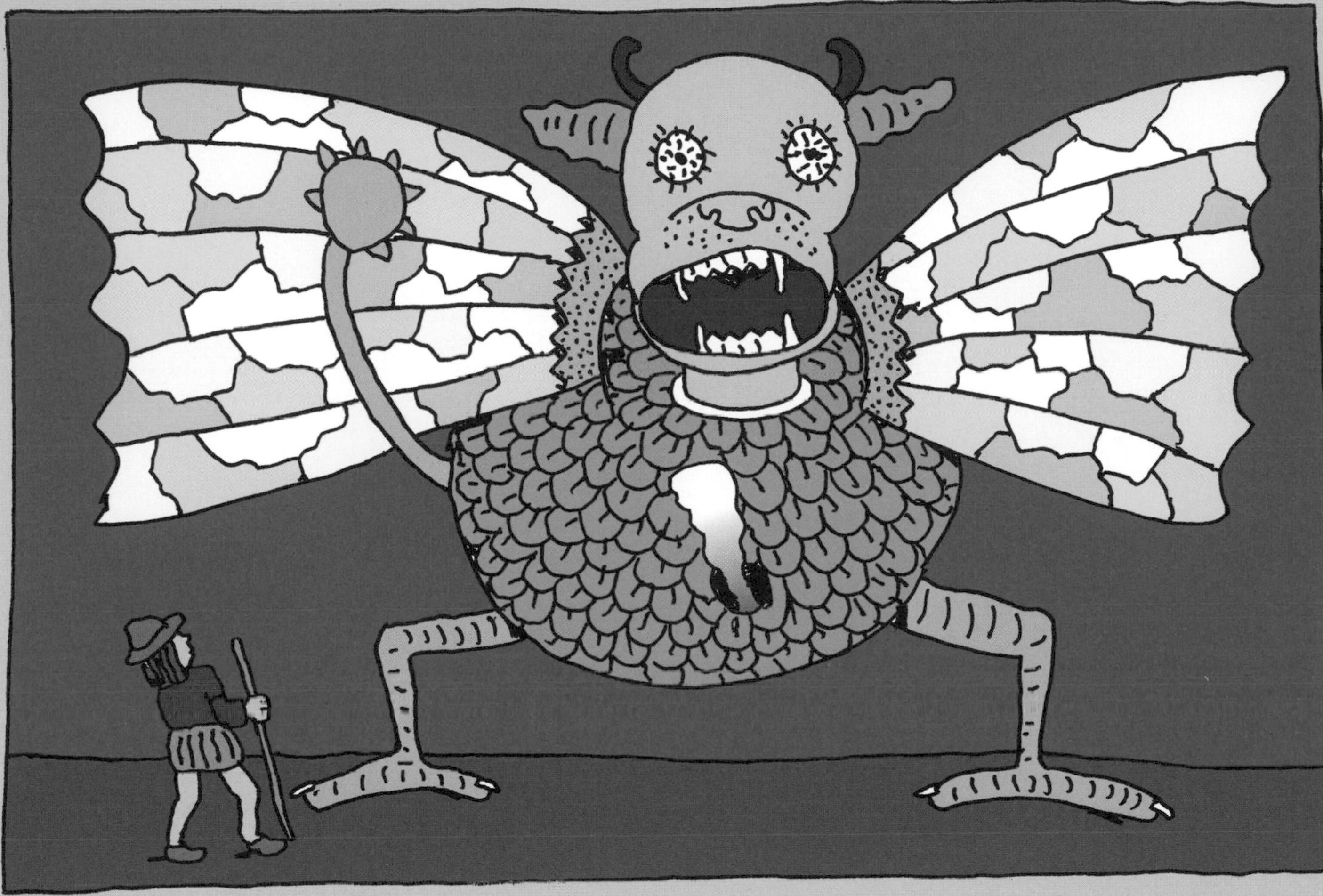

ISOBEL GOWDIE

Bored with monotonous life on the farm, Isobel Gowdie (c. 1610–1665) confessed practicing witchcraft and having intercourse with the devil, despite pain from a gigantic phallus. Her confessions in Scotland in 1662 were the most extraordinary at that time. At her trial she confessed to a witche's brew of beliefs and aberrations: they included secrets about mystic charms and admission she belonged to a coven that served the devil. The details of her satanic carnal interplay, including sucking her blood and bodily transformation with Satan, came to light too. She was the model of the modern ghoul.

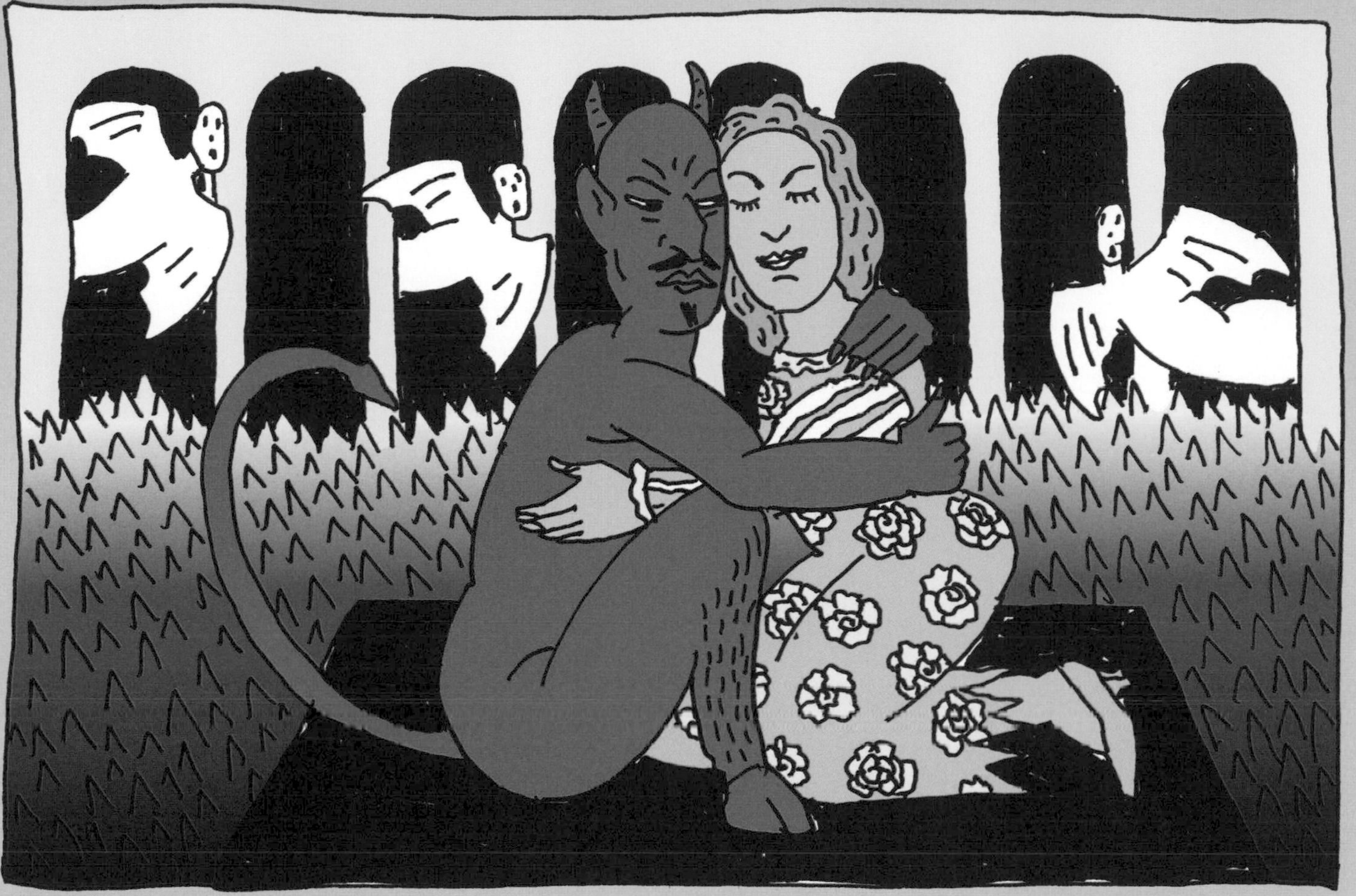

CHRISTOPH HAIZMANN'S SOUL

Haizmann, a failed painter in seventeenth-century Bavaria, claimed that he sold his soul to the Prince of Darkness in exchange for success. (Spoiler alert: don't do it.) After nine years Satan came for him, creating horrible visions which were also a recurrent subject for his paintings. It was said that the Virgin Mary interceded on his behalf, but disturbing visions persisted. The devil he saw had a human body with horns, a tail, female breasts and claws of a bird. Haizmann saw a cauldron with souls enduring flaming resin, sulfur and pitch. His case has been studied in psychology by Sigmund Freud.

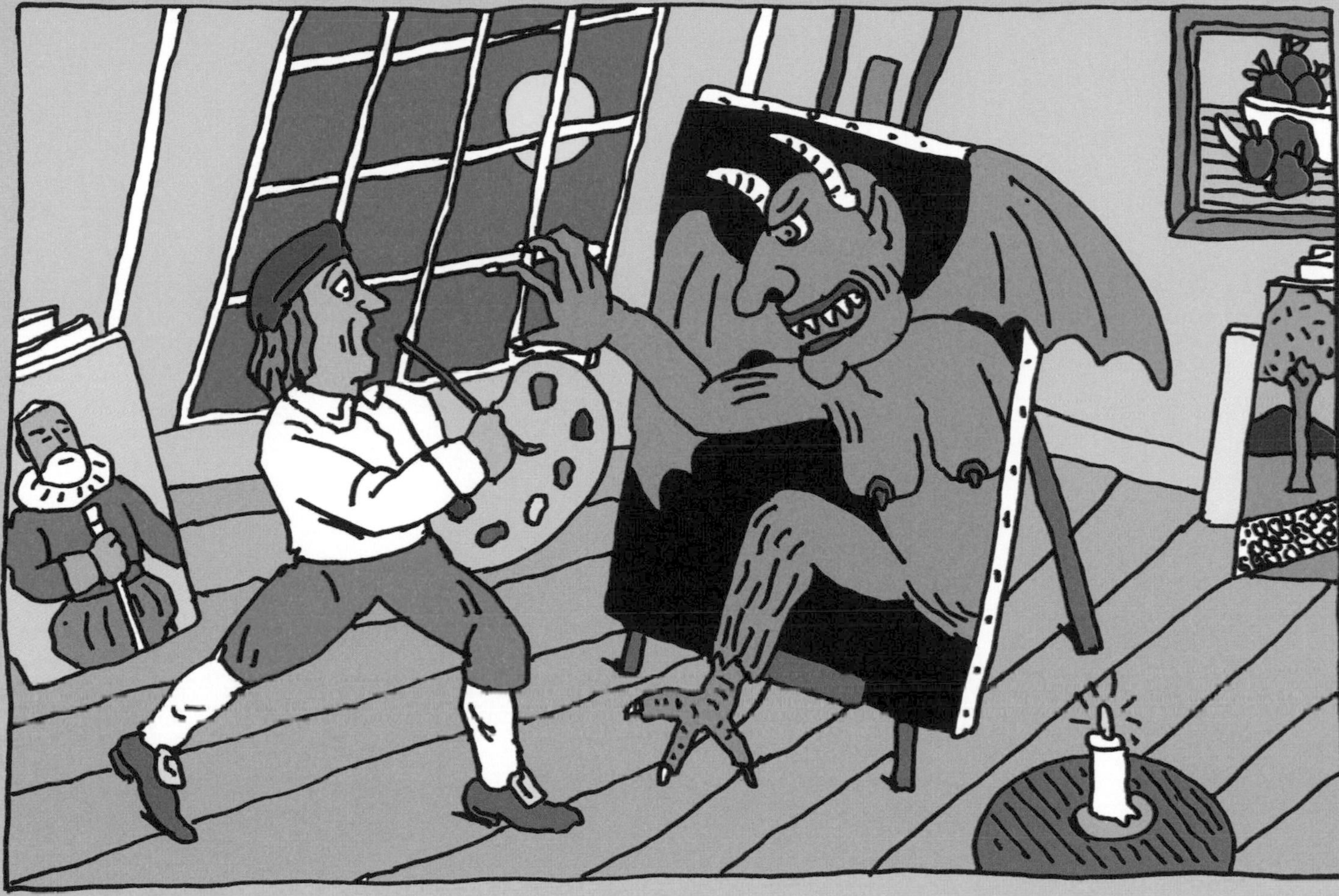

UNIVERSALISM AND SALVATION

Devoted to Jesus, Universalists are Christians who hold the belief that all humankind will be "saved," regardless of deeds in life. An early proponent was Origen Adamantius, a third-century theologian and Christian scholar, who couldn't believe that a loving God would save some people and doom the rest with eternal punishment. He maintained that punishment was only temporary and that it was a means to purify the soul. In more recent times, Universalists assert the use of reason also in religious matters, rejecting dogmatic elements of traditional Christianity in the light of scientific discoveries.

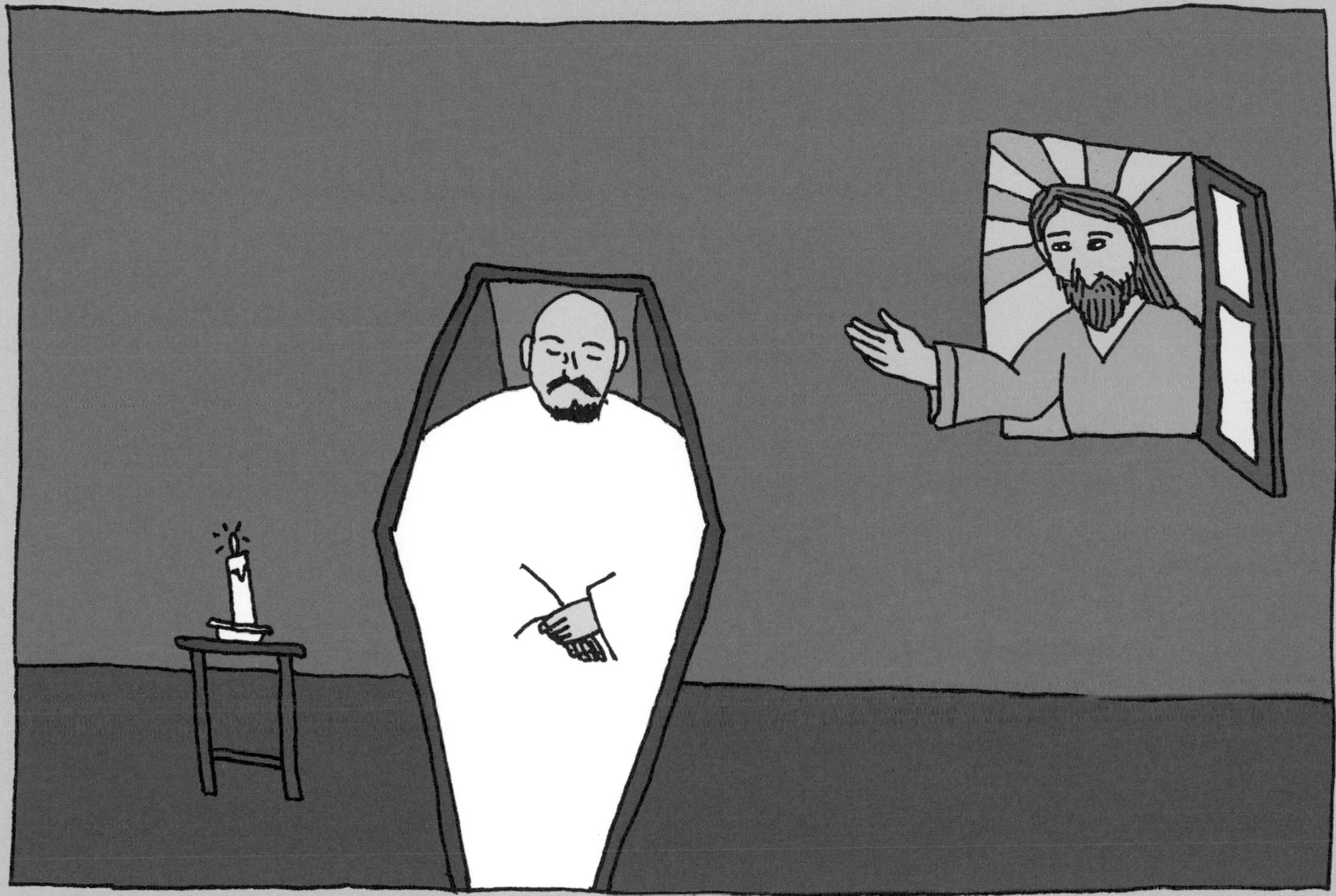

ell exists in the myths of many Asian and Asian Pacific rituals. The realm of the dead or "hell" in Chinese mythology is Diyu or "earth prison." Polynesian myths of the world beyond death are unsullied by the Christian idea of hell, which, differing from the old Judaic Sheol, was a place of punishment and torture for the wicked. Like all primitive hells or worlds of shadows, there is no morality in it; it is the place of the spirits of the dead, whether bad or good. What distinction there is lies between the aristocrats and the common people, who even in torment suffer inequities.

Diyu, Chinese Myths

There is a subterranean land called Diyu (meaning "earth prison") or Huángquán (the "yellow springs") that supposedly looks similar to our world above ground. But legend speaks of chambers where evildoers are torn in half, beheaded in pits of filth or climbing trees covered with sharp blades. The torture administered is matched according to the crimes committed during life. Luckily, merits earned during life with good deeds are taken into consideration. Souls are reincarnated and sent back above ground after being given a drink of forgetfulness.

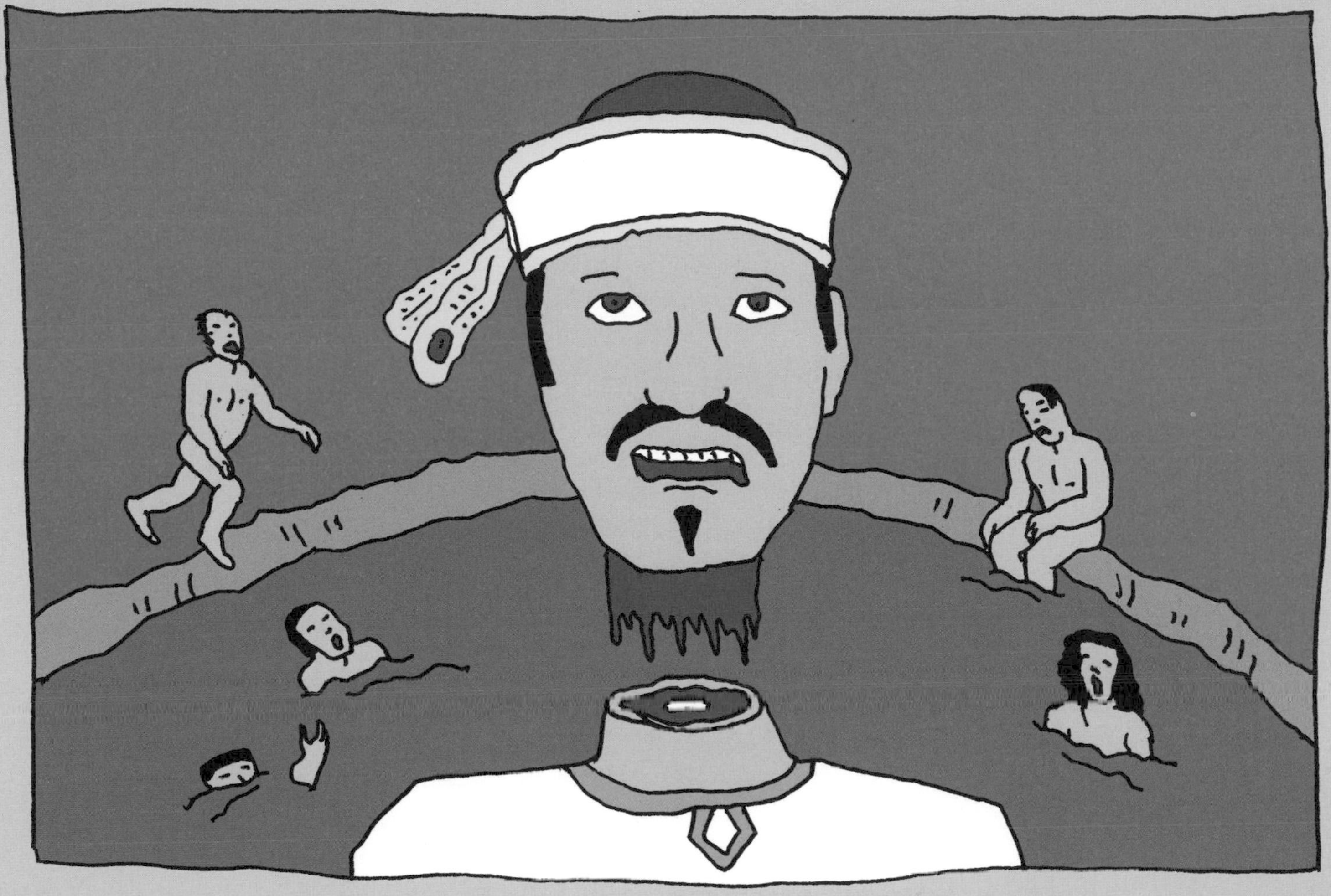

ENMA-Ō IN BUDDHISM

In the Japanese Buddhist tradition, Enma-ō is the ruler of the dead and master of hell. He judges the souls of men while his sister judges the souls of women, forcing them to look into mirrors that reflect the merit of each soul. Close by his side are two decapitated heads, which he relies on to peer further into the souls of sinners and judge them with some extra pairs of eyes. In Buddhism beings are not sent to hell as a divine punishment but as a direct result of their karma, the actions they took in life. Individuals are the only ones responsible for their fate. After a lengthy stay in Naraka, hell, beings are reborn in another realm, where they get another chance at living.

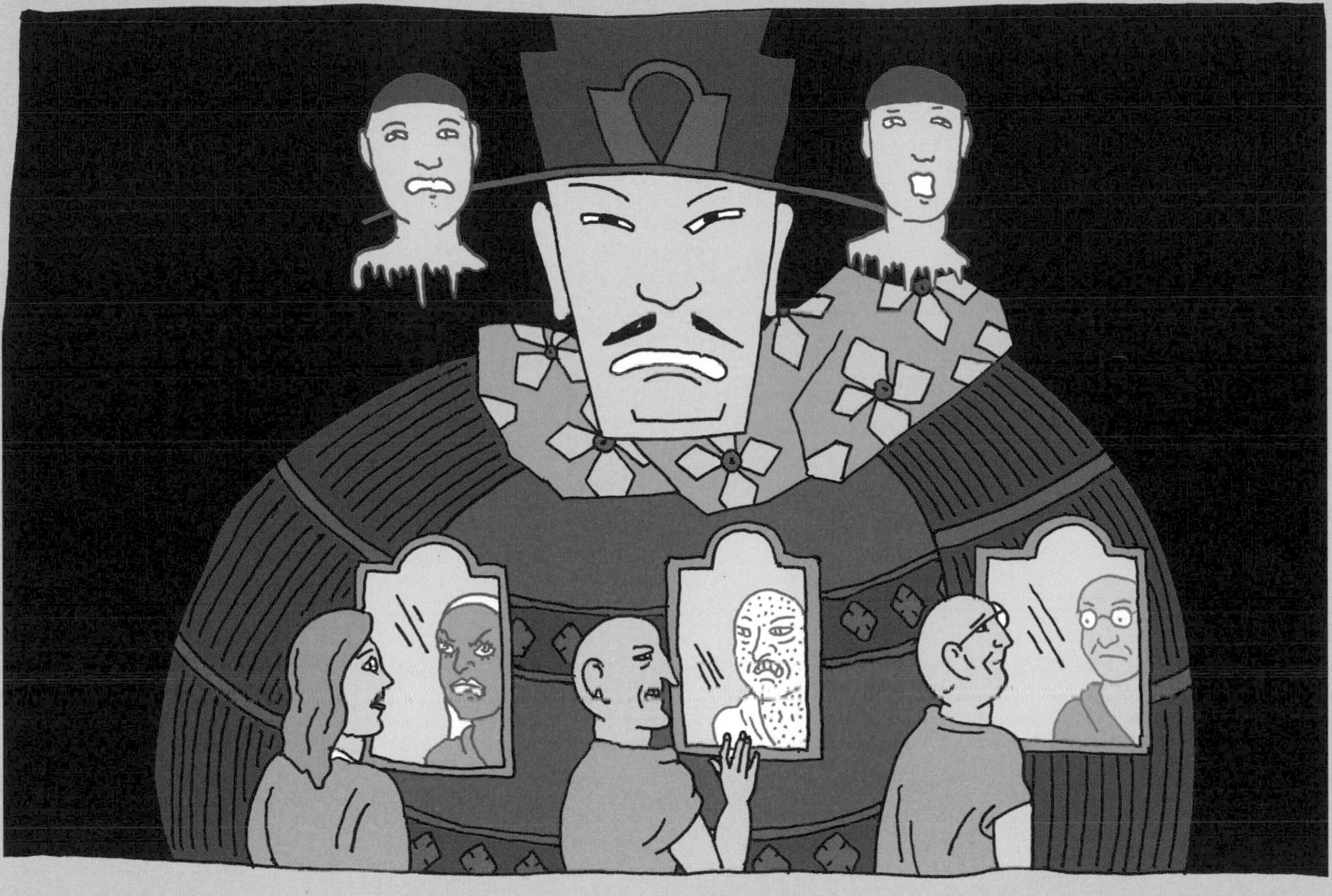

Buddhist Hell

Buddhist hell, Naraka, is comprised of sixteen layers, divided between hot and cold tortures. In the deepest circle of hell, the worst sinners are bludgeoned, forced to swallow hot coals, impaled with spears and hurled into lakes of fire. The smaller hells and their respective miseries include Boiling Excrement, Five Hundred Nails and Many Copper Cauldrons; others are called Stone Pestle, Pus and Blood, Axes and Hatchets and even Cold and Ice. Suffering is not eternal, though it is incomprehensibly long. It ranges from the time it would take to empty a barrel of sesame seeds at a single seed every hundred years to a full 2,560,000,000,000,000,000,000 years long.

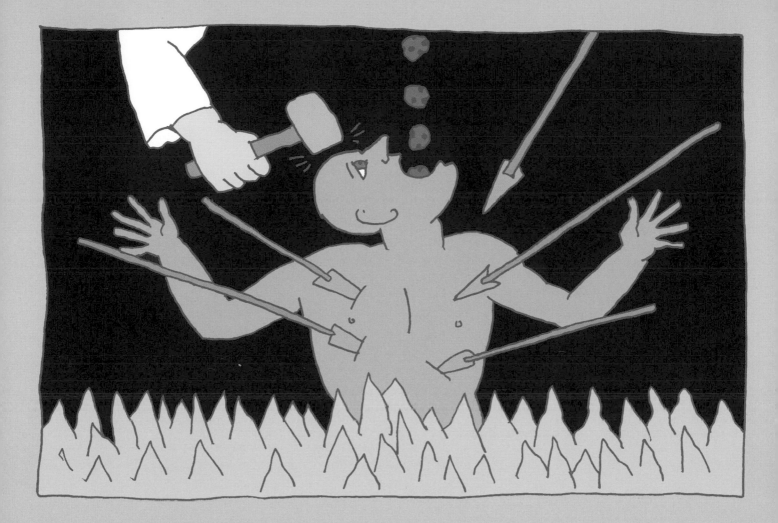

MOKUREN

In Japanese mythology, Mokuren is a Buddhist disciple. He learns that his mother is in the Hell of Hungry Spirits and is starving. He sends her some food but it turns to flame. Buddha tells him that she refused to feed a traveling priest. To obtain release Mokuren must feed every priest in the world on the fifteenth day of the seventh month. He succeeds with this task and his mother can take nourishment again. He is so happy he starts to dance, and today a traditional dance, Bon Odori, is still performed during the Bon festival, the Buddhist celebration of ancestors, when the spirits of the dead are believed to come back to visit.

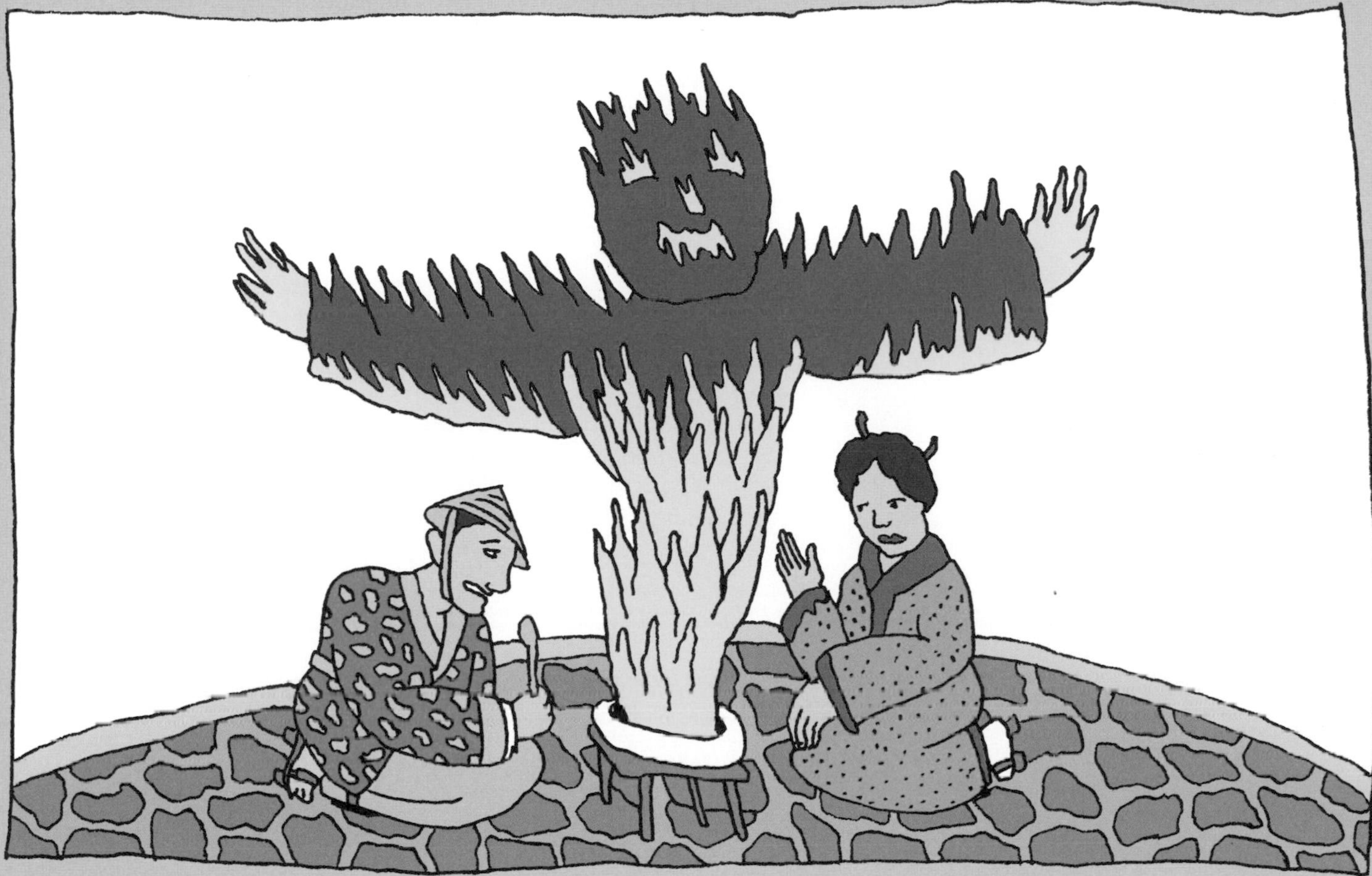

RAIKŌ

In Japanese mythology, Raikō, a valiant warrior, is blessed and hailed for his virtues. The people of Kyoto ask him to rid the city of its plague of demons but he is precipitously sickened. An ungodly fever brings on terrifying hallucinations of a fiery underworld. The resident demons engulf his body and seize his soul. In this manic state, Raikō is consumed by apparitions, especially a nightmarish mammoth spider whose aim is to trap and harm him. Yet like an ancient god or current superhero, Raikō miraculously conjures his sword and impales the spider. Raikō falls into a comatose sleep. When he awakens five days hence, the demons mystifyingly have vanished from Kyoto.

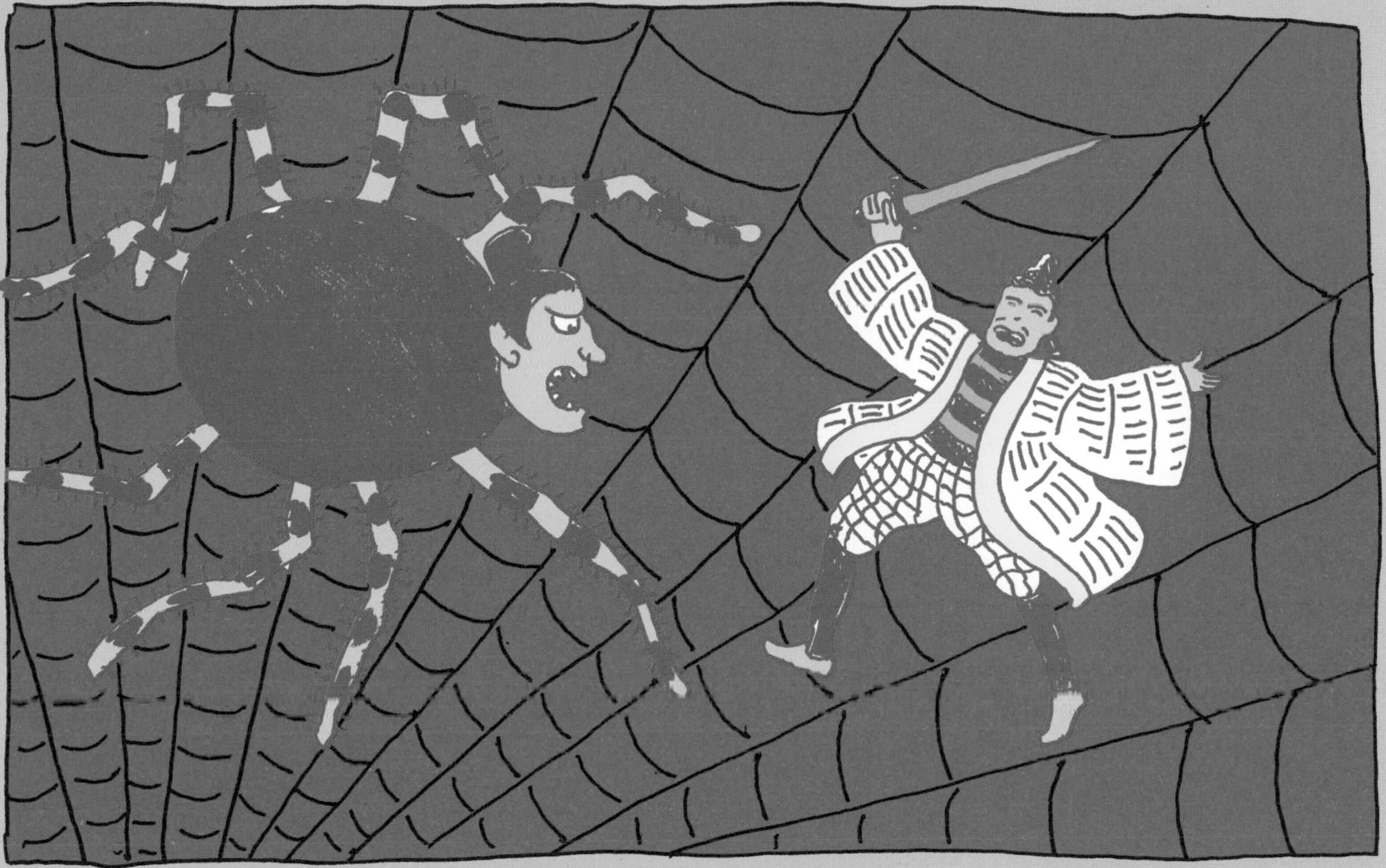

Jainism

According to the ancient Indian religion of Jainism, in Naraka (hell) there are 8.4 million torture chambers where a soul burns off bad karma, the spiritual residue of evil acts, until purified enough to be reborn into the infinite cycle of life. Each chamber has a specific demon to torture damned spirits according to their particular sins. Jains believe that the universe and everything in it is eternal. Nothing in it was created nor will it be destroyed. The universe consists of three realms: heaven, earth and hell.

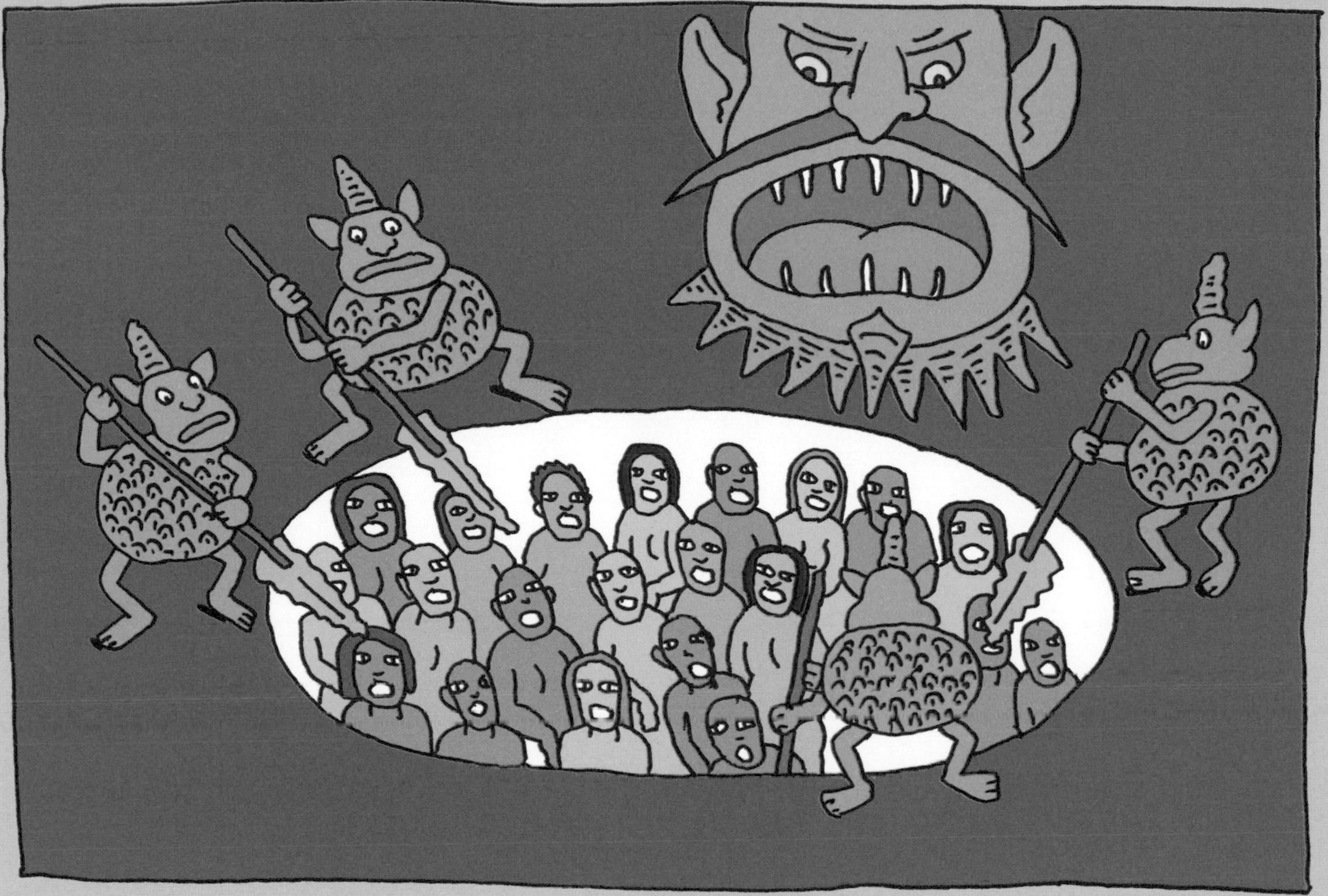

Shinto Underworld

Yomi, in Shinto mythology, is the "land of the dead." A dark realm, where all dead go regardless of their deeds in life, was believed to be beneath the earth. Izanami and Izanagi, her brother and also her former husband, are gods of creation and death. After Izanami's death, Izanagi travels to the underworld to bring her back. He doesn't know she has eaten the food of the dead and therefore cannot go back to the living world. When he sees she is a rotting, maggot-infested corpse, Izanagi escapes from Yomi and blocks the entrance with a large boulder, separating the realm of the living from the land of the dead, which he describes as a polluted land.

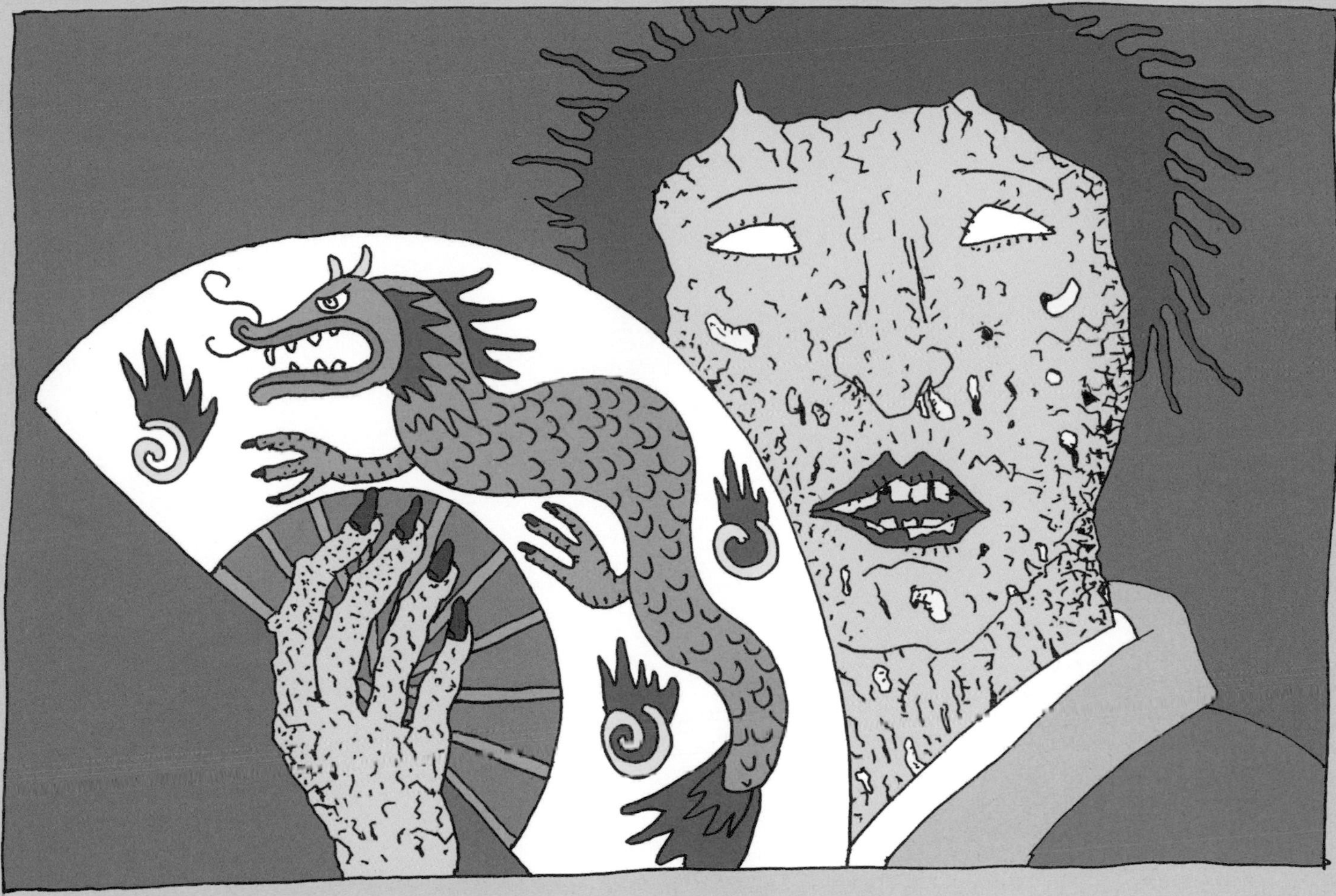

THE HINDU TRADITION

Yama presides over a courtroom-like hell. A record keeper named Chitragupta reads from a list of sinners and announces their sins for Yama to determine the appropriate punishment: swimming in boiling oil, burning in fire or suffering torture with weapons. Once individuals meet their quota of torture, they get to be reborn back onto earth with their balance of karma.

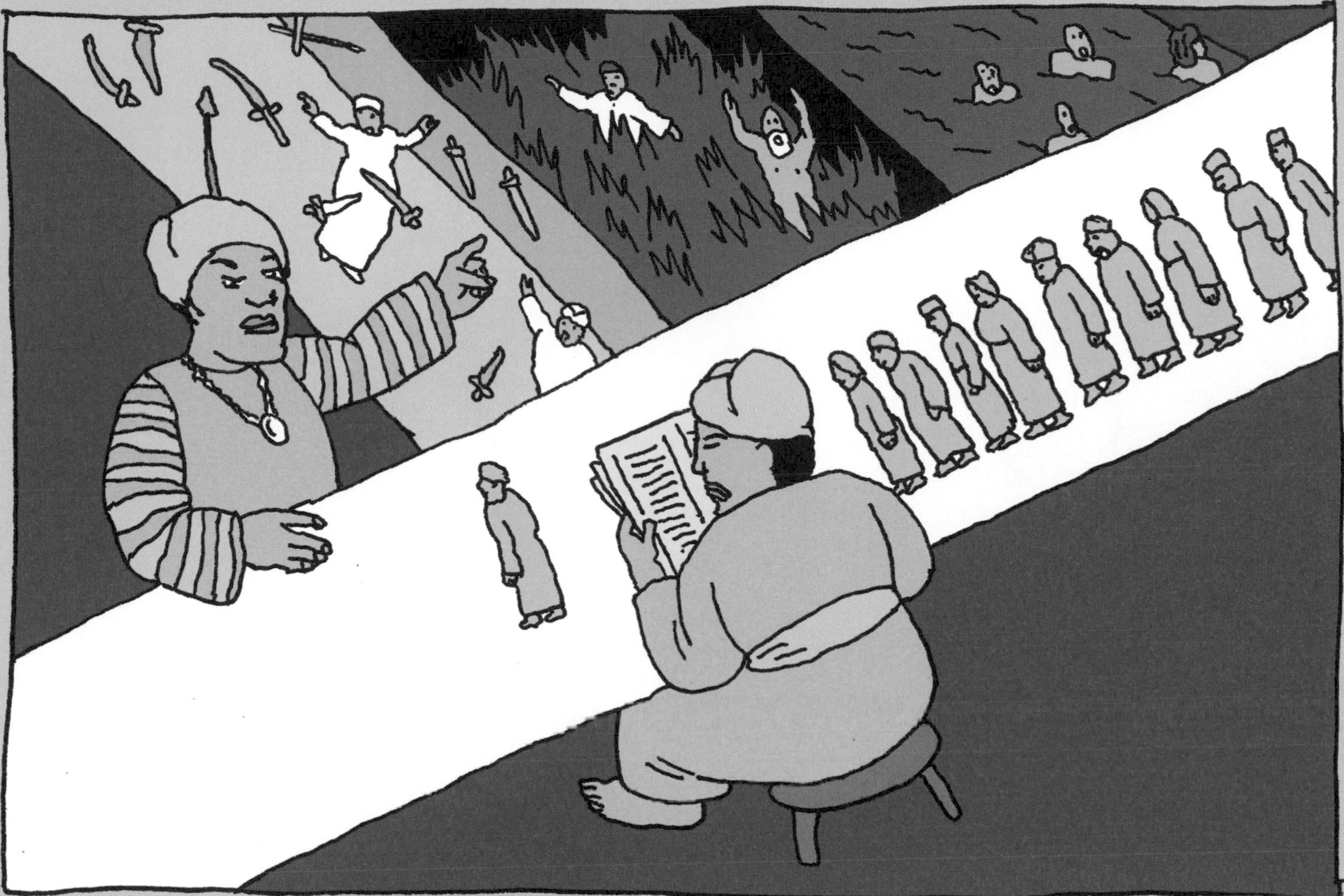

SIKHISM

There is no heaven or hell. According to Arjan, one of the Sikh gurus who lived in the sixteenth century, people who are entangled in emotional attachment are living in hell on earth. Heaven and hell are places in the hereafter; they are spiritual, not existential. The reference is to a person's good and evil physical life on earth. So, the duality of afterlife plays no role in Sikh belief. Truthful living in the noble fear of life is heaven, while no faith in God and living an immoral life is ostensibly hell. Apart from one's own hallucinations, in reality the lord of death (or god or demon) does not exist.

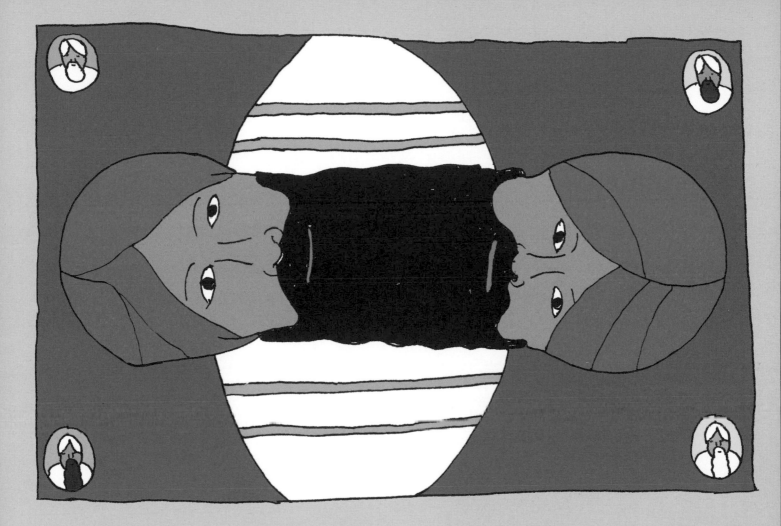

Tibetan Book of the Dead

In Tibet, Nepal and Mongolia, a lama (spiritual teacher) will often recite the *Book of the Dead* to a recently deceased person to help him understand his experiences and gain enlightenment. It chronicles various stages while dying, and the forty-nine-day interval between death and rebirth. Composed in the eighth century by Padmasambhava, a mythical Buddhist guru—who concealed the book because the world was not ready for its teaching—it tells of Yama, the god of death, who beheads and removes the heart and intestines of the evil ones.

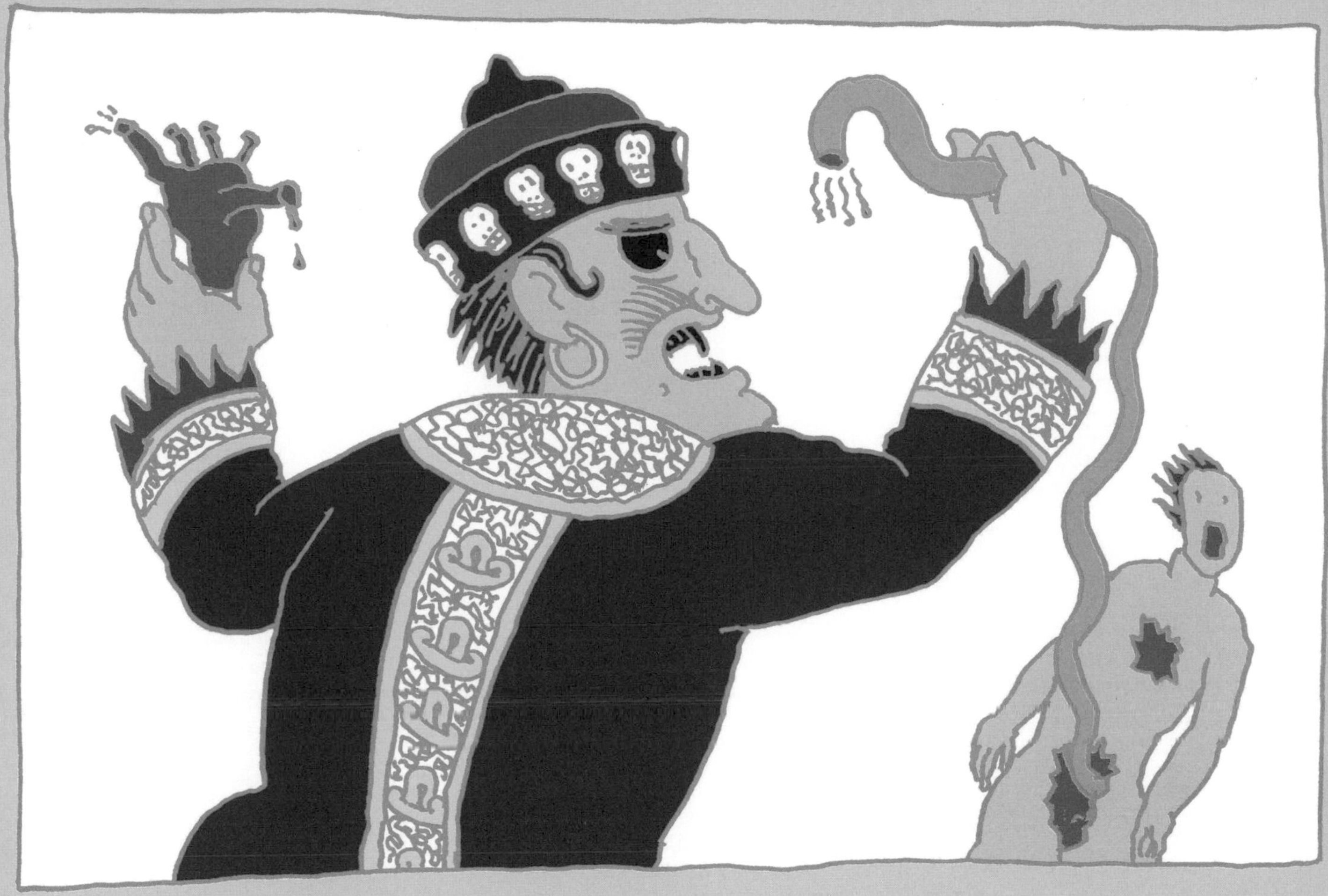

Mu Monto

Legendary hero of Siberian mythology, Mu Monto travels to the underworld to retrieve a stallion he had sacrificed on the occasion of his father's funeral. He is led by a black fox to the portals of the underworld. Mu Monto enters and finds liars' lips sewn together, a wealthy woman who must wear rags and a poor woman who now enjoys great luxury.

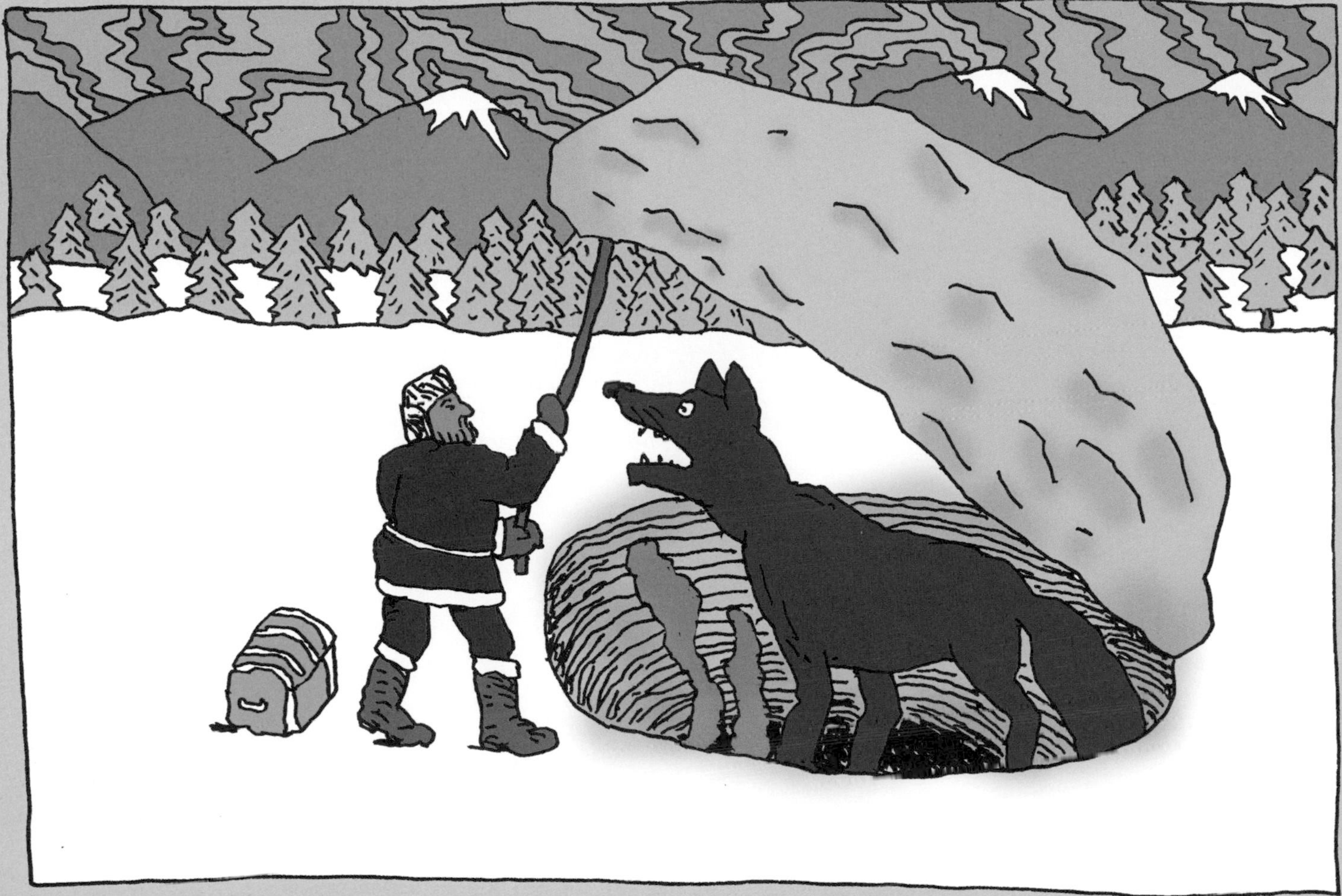

KANALOA: HAWAIIAN MYTHOLOGY

Kanaloa is considered to be the god of the Islands' lurid underworld, as well as of evil and death, and is a teacher of magic. He is in conflict with good deities like Kāne, the highest of the four major gods, and the creator of life. Kanaloa and Kāne complement and oppose each other. Kanaloa and his spirits rebelled against the other gods and were sent to the underworld as a punishment, in a myth similar to Christian Lucifer. In the traditions of ancient Hawaii, Kanaloa is symbolized by a squid or octopus.

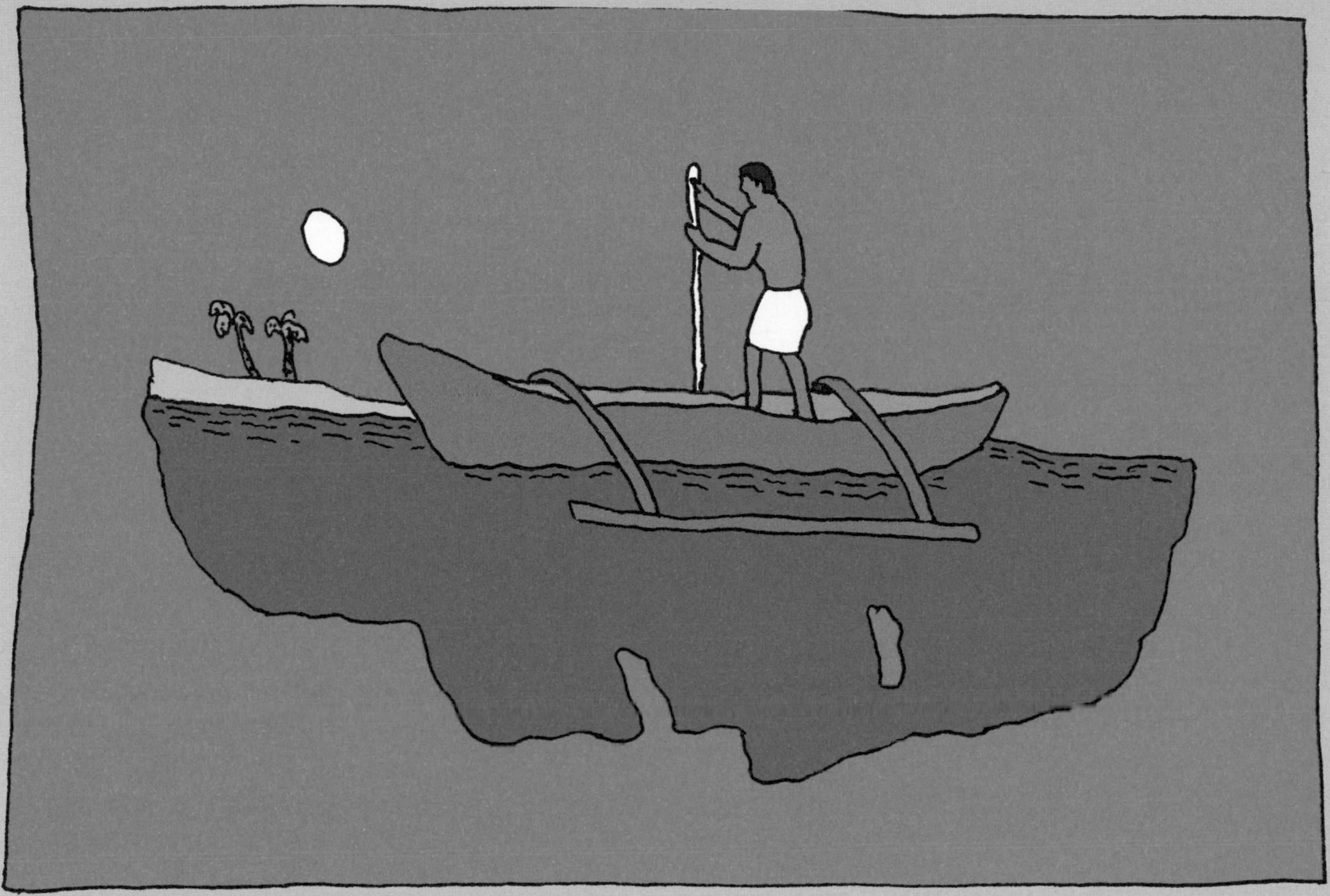

Myths of The Caroline Islands

Gora-Daileng is the lord of the dead. His tortures include boiling spirits in a hot furnace and casting them in an endless river. In this way depraved souls are punished. The strong current carries them away.

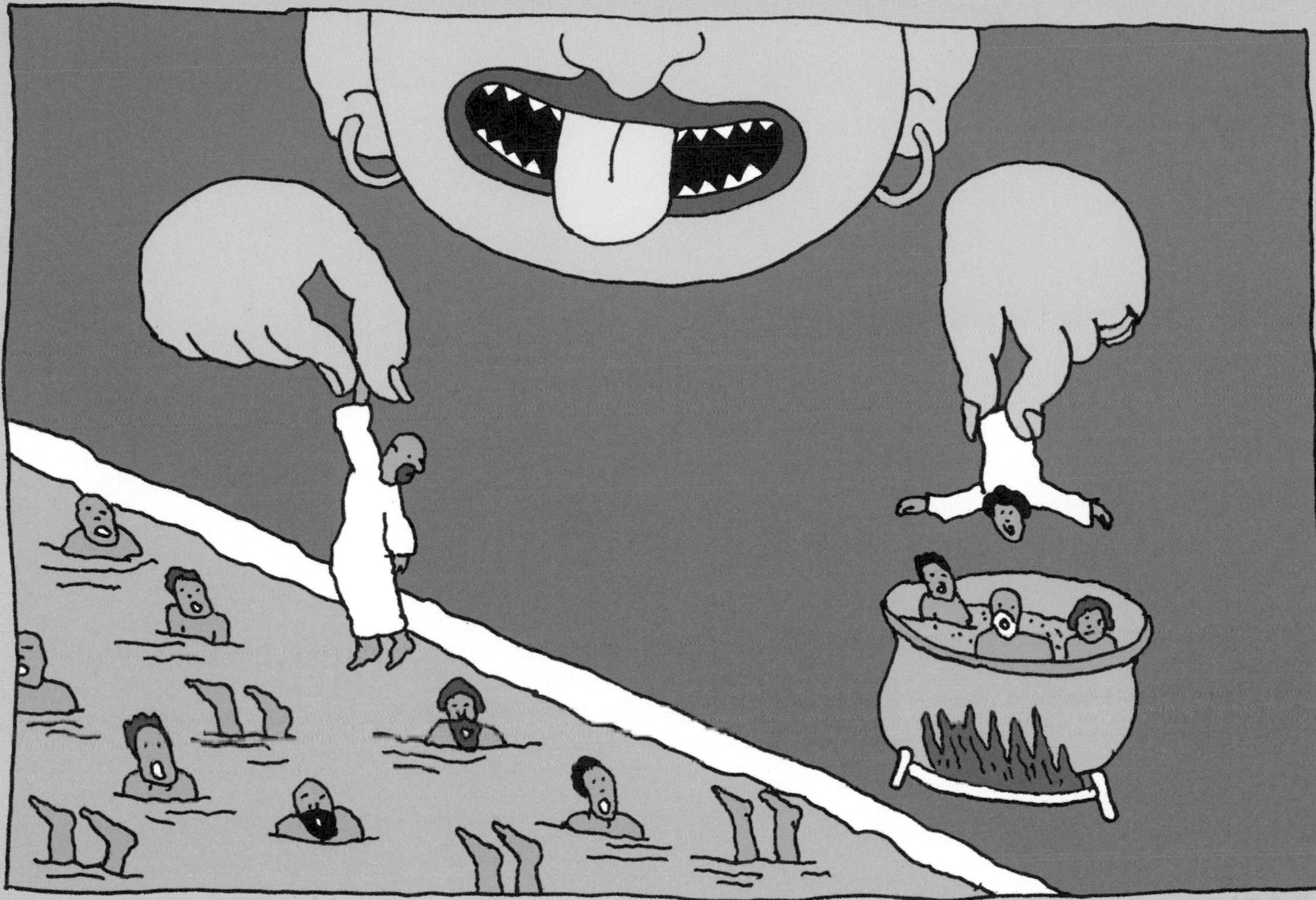

DEDICATION

Dedicated to Saints and Sinners.

ACKNOWLEDGMENTS

The authors wish to give thanks to Camille (Millie) Murphy for her blood, sweat and smiles.

AND TO THE AUTHORS OF THE FOLLOWING:

Encyclopedia of Hell, by Miriam Van Scott. St. Martin's Griffin, New York, 1999 (first edition).

The Bible of the World, edited by Robert O. Ballou, Friedrich Spiegelberg and Horace L. Friess. K. Paul Trench Trübner & Co. Ltd., London, 1946 (third edition).

The History of Hell, by Alice K. Turner. Houghton Mifflin Harcourt, New York, 1998.

The Tibetan Book of the Dead: First Complete Translation. Penguin Classics, London, 2007.

Dante's Divine Comedy: A Graphic Adaptation, by Seymour Chwast. Bloomsbury, New York, 2007.

Jimbo's Inferno, by Gary Panter. Fantagraphics, Seattle, 2006.

The Devil Wears Prada, by Lauren Weisberger. Random House, New York, 2004.

Published by
Princeton Architectural Press
A division of Chronicle Books LLC
70 West 36th Street, New York, NY 10018
papress.com

© 2023 Seymour Chwast (artwork)
© 2023 Steven Heller (text)
© Maurizio Corraini srl 2023
All rights reserved to Maurizio Corraini srl Mantova.

First Italian edition by Maurizio Corraini srl 2022

American English translation license authorized by Maurizio Corraini srl Mantova Italy

Printed and bound in China
26 25 24 23   4 3 2 1 First edition

ISBN 978-1-7972-2561-6

Library of Congress Control Number: 2023932859

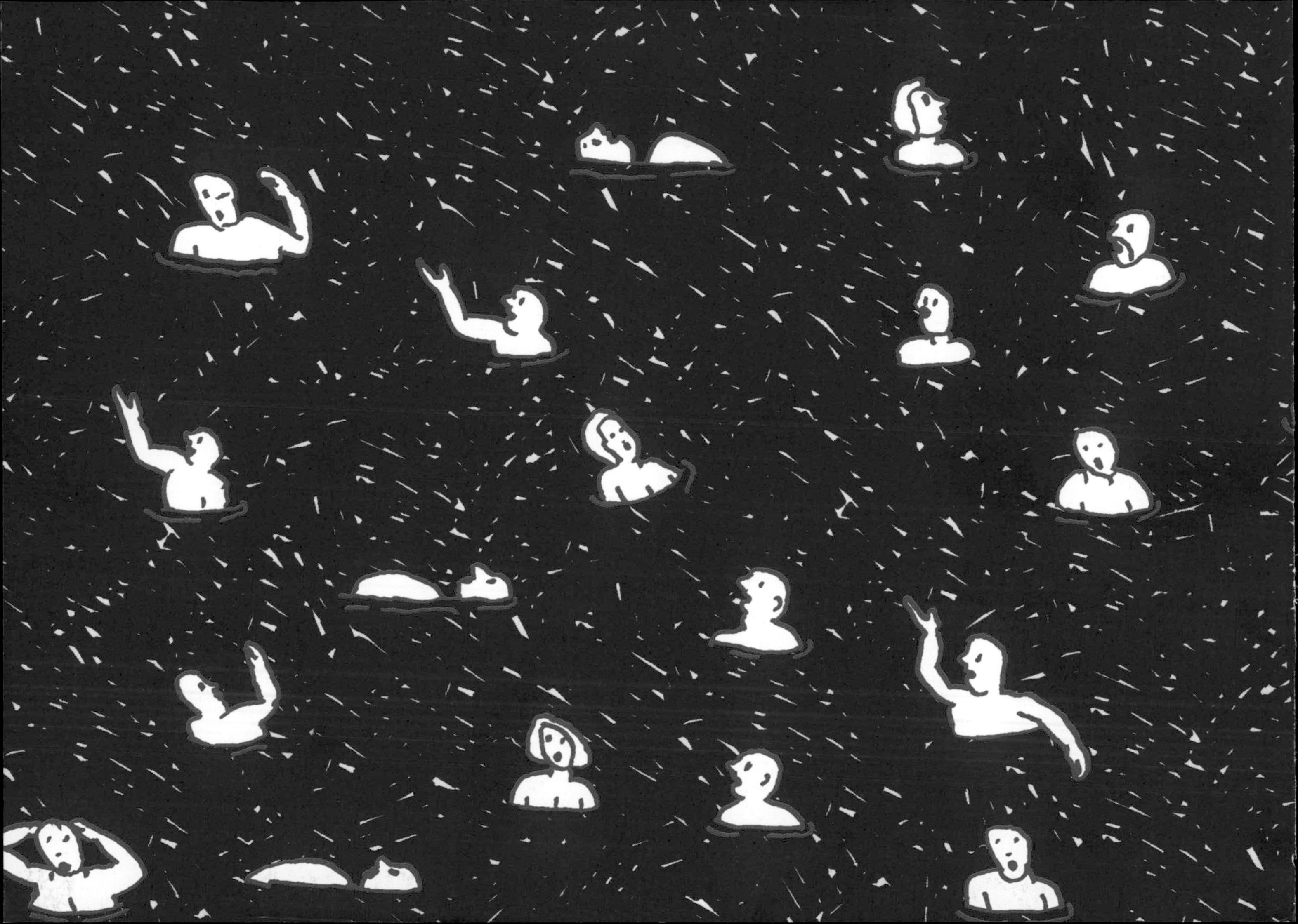